LAWRENCE BRODY AND DONALD O. JANSEN

Leveraging Life Insurance Premium Payments

Second Edition

USING SPLIT-DOLLAR AND RELATED PARTY PREMIUM FINANCING TECHNIQUES

ABA
AMERICANBARASSOCIATION
Real Property, Trust and Estate Law Section

Cover design by Andrew Alcala

Library of Congress Cataloging-in-Publication Data
Names: Brody, Lawrence, 1942- author. | Jansen, Donald O., author.
Title: Leveraging life insurance premium payments : using split-dollar and related party premium financing techniques / Lawrence Brody, Donald Jansen.
Description: [Second edition]. | Chicago : American Bar Association, 2025. | Includes bibliographical references and index. | Summary: "With the effective date of the Final Split-Dollar Regulations in 2003, many commentators asserted that split-dollar premium financing was dead. A reader of this book should be persuaded that these predictions were indeed premature. Although split-dollar arrangements have significantly changed from the grandfathered split-dollar rules (although in many ways they have remained the same), such arrangements are very much alive today-they are not dead, merely different. Particularly with premium loans, practitioners (to their peril) may not realize that they are involved with the split-dollar regimes when financing life insurance premium payments. Hopefully this book will serve as an useful guide in providing for leveraging life insurance premium payments, whichever regime is used"--Provided by publisher.
Identifiers: LCCN 2025002918 (print) | LCCN 2025002919 (ebook) | ISBN 9781639056163 (hardback) | ISBN 9781639056170 (epub)
Subjects: LCSH: Life insurance--Law and legislation--United States. | Insurance premiums--Law and legislation--United States. | Insurance premiums--Finance--Law and legislation--United States.
Classification: LCC KF1175 .B76 2025 (print) | LCC KF1175 (ebook) | DDC 346.73/08632--dc23
LC record available at https://lccn.loc.gov/2025002918
LC ebook record available at https://lccn.loc.gov/2025002919

Printed in the United States of America.

29 28 27 26 25   5 4 3 2 1

Discounts are available for books ordered in bulk. Special consideration is given to state bars, CLE programs, and other bar-related organizations. Inquire at Book Publishing, ABA Publishing, American Bar Association, 321 N. Clark Street, Chicago, Illinois 60654-7598.

www.shopABA.org

Contents

About the Authors

Lawrence Brody

Lawrence Brody is Senior Counsel at Harrison LLP, residing in their St. Louis office, and is a member of the Missouri Bar. He retired as an adjunct professor at Washington University School of Law, after 50 years of teaching Estate Planning and Drafting. He is a visiting adjunct professor at the University of Miami Law School, teaching a course on life insurance. He is the author or co-author of numerous articles and books on the use of life insurance in estate and employee benefit planning, including two BNA Tax Management Portfolios, two books for the National Underwriter Company, and a number of volumes in the ABA Insurance Counselor Series.

Mr. Brody has been a frequent presenter for American Law Institute CLE estate planning programs, Society of Financial Professionals programs, major life insurance industry programs (including the MDRT, LIMRA, the Top of the Table, AALU and the International Forum), the Heckerling Institute, the Notre Dame Estate Planning Conference, the Southern Federal Tax Institute, the NYU Tax Institute, the NAEPC Annual Meeting, and regional and annual ACTEC conferences.

Mr. Brody is a member of The American College of Trust and Estate Counsel (ACTEC), an emeritus member of the Advisory Committee for the Philip E. Heckerling Institute on Estate Planning (University of Miami School of Law), and a member of the Editorial Board of the Society of Financial Service Professionals CLU Journal. He received the designation of Accredited Estate Planner by the National Association of Estate Planners and Councils and was one of 10 individuals awarded its Distinguished Accredited Estate Planner designation in the initial class (2004). He has been named in the Private Wealth Law Section of Chambers High Net Worth Guide. Mr. Brody was named a Distinguished Law Alumni by Washington University School of Law in 2012.

Donald O. Jansen is Associate General Counsel, University of Texas System Office of General Counsel. He is a retired senior partner of Fulbright & Jaworski LLP (now Norton Rose Fulbright). He is a former fellow of the American College of Trust and Estate Counsel and a current fellow of the American College of Tax Counsel. Mr. Jansen is a past chairman of the Committee of Significant Current Literature and Vice Chair of the Insurance Committee, Probate and Trust Division, Real Property, Probate and Trust Law Section of the American Bar Association. Mr. Jansen is a specialist in estate planning and probate law certified by the Texas Board of Legal Specialization and is the past probate editor of the *Newsletter of the Real Estate, Probate and Trust Law Section* of the State Bar of Texas. He was designated by his peers as a Texas Super Lawyer in estate planning in 2003, 2004, and 2005. He is a 2014 recipient of the Outstanding Eagle Scout Award presented by the National Association of Eagle Scouts. He is a past member of the Federal Bar Association National Council and a past president of the Houston Chapter. Mr. Jansen was elected to the Estate Planning Hall of Fame in 2017 by the National Association of Estate Planners & Councils. He is an Accredited Estate Planner (Distinguished). Mr. Jansen is a member of the Advisory Committee, Heckerling Institute on Estate Planning, University of Miami School of Law.

I. An Overview of Split-Dollar Premium Financing

Split-dollar financing of life insurance premium payments has been around for more than 80 years. It is useful in any situation when one person or entity has the cash to pay the premiums and another person or entity has the need for life insurance coverage. Originally, split-dollar arrangements were used in the employment and shareholder context; the objective was to allow the employee or shareholder to acquire the policy for a lower premium or tax cost than without the arrangement. The policy premiums, death benefits, and cash value were split between the parties (hence the name). Normally, the employer's or corporation's share of the death benefit or cash value was designed to reimburse it for the premium payments made under the arrangement, without interest. The employer would assist the employee in obtaining life insurance coverage by paying all or part of the insurance premiums. In the shareholder context, the corporation would help one or more of its shareholders obtain life insurance, quite often to help finance a cross-purchase stock agreement.

In more recent years, split-dollar arrangements have been used in a wealth transfer context—the insurance policy is split between an irrevocable life insurance trust (ILIT) and the employer or corporation or, in a private split-dollar arrangement, the donor. This allows the annual gift to the ILIT to be much less than the entire premium payment because the employer, corporation, or donor was entitled to recover its advances from the cash value or death benefit.

The current split-dollar rules came into effect with the final split-dollar regulations, effective September 18, 2003 (the Final Split-Dollar Regulations or the Regulations). For historical reasons, before that date, the Internal Revenue Service (IRS) had taken the position that the arrangement was not a loan but an investment by the employer, corporation, or donor. This was true whether the premium payer owned the policy under the endorsement method with all or part of the pure death benefit endorsed to the employee, shareholder, or ILIT or under the collateral assignment method where the policy was owned by the employee, shareholder, or an ILIT, with the policy cash value and death benefits securing repayment of the premiums advanced by the premium payer. As will be discussed later, these rules still apply to life insurance split-dollar arrangements grandfathered from the Final Split-Dollar Regulations. Under the Regulations, however, most (but not all) collateral assignment arrangements will be taxed under the loan regime, and all endorsement arrangements will be taxed under the economic benefit regime, with considerably different tax and ownership consequences. But in either case, the cash value and death proceeds are still split between the premium payer and the other party.

This book discusses the peculiar rules for both of the premium financing regimes and the tax consequences and planning techniques of each. The tax and other issues affecting split-dollar arrangements grandfathered from the Final Split-Dollar Regulations are also analyzed.

II. Preliminary Matters

A. Premium Financing and Split-Dollar Terminology

In today's parlance, after the Final Split-Dollar Regulations became effective, "private" or "related party" premium financing refers to financing life insurance premium payments through loans to the owner of the policy (e.g., the insured, shareholder, or employee; a trust; or a family member) from an employer, a corporation, a partnership, the insured, or a family member. Under the Final Split-Dollar Regulations, such loans fall within the loan regime subject to the tax rules specified in the Section 7872 Regulation.[1]

If the premium payer also owns the policy with all or part of the death benefit and perhaps other policy rights endorsed to the insured, shareholder, or employee; a trust; or a family member, the arrangement is often referred to as *endorsement split-dollar*. The Final Split-Dollar Regulations treat this type of arrangement under the economic benefit regime, subject to the tax rules specified in the Section 61 Regulation.[2]

Although both the loan regime and the economic benefit regime are split-dollar arrangements, this booklet often refers to the loan regime as *premium financing* and the economic benefit regime sometimes as *economic benefit split-dollar* or as *endorsement split-dollar*. It should be noted that if the premium financing loans are from an independent party such as a bank, those loans are not subject to Section 7872 if they are made available by the lender to the general public on the same terms and conditions and that are consistent with the lender's customary business practice.[3] Even if the third-party loan does not fall within this commercial loan exception (e.g., the particular loan is negotiated with unique terms), though technically subject to the loan regime, there will normally be neither income tax nor gift tax consequences because the market interest rate charged by the lender for the loan will probably exceed the applicable federal rate (AFR).[4] This book does not discuss such third-party loans but focuses on private or related party premium financing.

B. Generally, What Is a Split-Dollar Arrangement—Whether Loan Regime or Economic Benefit Regime?

Generally, under the Regulations, a split-dollar life insurance arrangement is an arrangement between an "owner" and a "non-owner" of a life insurance contract that satisfies the following criteria:[5]

(1) Either party to the arrangement pays, directly or indirectly, all or a portion of the premiums on the life insurance contract, including a payment by means of a loan to the other party that is secured by the life insurance contract.

(2) At least one of the parties to the arrangement paying the premiums is entitled to recover (conditionally or unconditionally) all or any portion of those premiums, and such recovery is to be made from, or is secured by, the proceeds of the life insurance contract.

(3) The arrangement is not part of a group-term life insurance plan described in Section 79 unless the group-term life insurance plan provides permanent benefits to the employees.[6]

Certain compensatory and shareholder arrangements will be treated as split-dollar life insurance arrangements even though they don't meet all of the requirements of the general rule, if the following conditions are met:[7]

(1) The arrangement is entered into in connection with the performance of services and is not part of a group-term life insurance plan described in Internal Revenue Code (the Code) Section 79 or is between a corporation and another person in that person's capacity as a shareholder in the corporation.

(2) The employer or service recipient or the corporation pays, directly or indirectly, all or any portion of the premium.

(3) The beneficiary of all or part of any portion of the death benefit is designated by the employee or service provider or by the shareholder or is any person whom the employee or service provider or shareholder would reasonably be expected to designate as the beneficiary, or the employee or service provider or the shareholder has any interest in the policy cash value of the life insurance contract. These types of arrangements are referred to as "undocumented," "unsecured," or "sole owner" split-dollar arrangements.

There have been several cases involving compensatory split-dollar arrangements between employer created welfare benefit trusts under Section 419 owning insurance policies on employee lives in which the employer was not reimbursed out of policy cash value.[8]

Thus, a compensatory or shareholder split-dollar arrangement falls within the Regulation definition even though the recovery of premiums by the employer or corporation does not come from, nor is secured by, the policy cash value. Why would a corporation or an employer draft a split-dollar arrangement without requiring that premium recovery be from, or secured by, the policy cash value? A probable reason is to avoid the estate tax attribution rule of incidents of ownership of a policy owned by a corporation to an insured controlling shareholder.[9] Note that a non-compensatory split-dollar arrangement must meet the general definition requiring that the premiums be recovered from, or secured by, the policy proceeds to be subject to the Regulations.

Although the Final Split-Dollar Regulations provide rules for split-dollar arrangements involving employees, shareholders, and private split-dollar arrangements, the Regulations reserve without comment split-dollar arrangements with partners for policies owned by a partnership.[10]

C. Under the Regulations, the Policy Owner Generally Determines Whether the Loan Regime or the Economic Benefit Regime Applies

If the employer, corporation, service recipient, or donor is the owner of the life insurance contract subject to the split-dollar arrangement, the endorsement economic benefit regime applies.[11]

If the employee, shareholder, donee, or any other person owns the life insurance contract subject to the split-dollar arrangement, the loan regime applies (with one important exception, discussed later).[12] Stated another way, if the employer, corporation, or donor is not the policy owner, the loan regime applies. Accordingly, the loan regime is the default regime. The employer or service recipient is attributed ownership of a compensatory split-dollar arrangement if the owner is an employee or service recipient created 402(b) trust, a grantor trust, or a welfare benefit plan under Section 419(e)(1)(iii) or is a member of the employer or service recipient's controlled group or a trade or business that is under common control.[13]

How is the owner identified? With respect to a life insurance contract, the person named as the policy owner of such contract is generally the owner of such contract for determination of the applicable regime under the Regulations. The "non-owner" is any other person who has direct or indirect interest in the contract.[14] If two or more persons are named as policy owners of a life insurance contract:[15]

(1) But each person does not have, at all times, all incidents of ownership with respect to an undivided interest in the contract, the person who is the first-named policy owner is treated as the owner of the entire contract OR

(2) Each person has, at all times, all of the incidents of ownership with respect to an undivided interest in the contract, each person is treated as the owner of a separate contract to the extent of such person's undivided interest. In such a situation, there would be no split-dollar arrangement with regard to either portion of the contract.

As noted earlier, there is a special, important exception to the named owner rule, which is especially useful in an estate planning context. Even if the employee or donee is listed as owner of the life insurance contract subject to the split-dollar arrangement, the employer, service recipient, or donor will be treated as the owner under the endorsement economic benefit regime rather than having the loan regime apply if (and only if) the only economic benefit to the employee or donee is the current life insurance protection.[16] This is called non-equity split-dollar because the premium payer is entitled to all of the cash value. Note that this exception does not apply to corporation, shareholder, or other types of split-dollar arrangements.

When would a non-equity split-dollar arrangement be used? Again, it would be used for estate tax planning purposes. If the donor were the insured or the employer was a corporation and the insured employee were the controlling shareholder, under the general rule, to use the economic benefit regime, the donor, employer, or corporation would have to be owner of the policy, which would give the deceased insured incidents of ownership under Section 2042.[17] To prevent control of the cash value by the insured donor or by a controlled corporation with direct or attributed incidents of ownership to the deceased insured, a bare bones or restricted collateral assignment in favor of the employer, corporation, or donor should be used to give all incidents of ownership to the non-owner, retaining for the premium payer only the right to receive the greater of the premiums advanced or the policy cash value at termination of the arrangement.[18]

D. Other Premium Payment Possibilities

It should be noted that there may be other ways to pay premiums without use of endorsement split-dollar or premium financing even when one person pays the premiums and another owns the policy. However, these alternatives may have their advantages and disadvantages compared with split-dollar arrangements. A donor insured might make outright gifts to an individual or an ILIT without gift tax consequences by use of gift tax annual exclusions or the applicable exclusion amount. An employer might pay the premium on a policy on the employee's life with the employee owning the policy and with the premiums subject to income tax to the employee under Section 162 Executive Bonus Plans. If third-party ownership is required for wealth transfer free from estate taxes, perhaps the policy can be bought by an existing ILIT, family partnership, or family limited liability company with sufficient assets to pay the premiums but with little or no ownership by the insured in the purchasing entity.

E. Split-Dollar Financing Is Temporary, Particularly for ILIT Purposes

There are several ways to develop permanent ILIT premium payments for an ILIT that has few other assets.

1. Outright Gifts

The use of outright gifts is the simplest method with fewer gift, estate, and generation-skipping transfer (GST) tax issues. However, to avoid gift tax consequences, this method is limited to the gift tax unified credit with its applicable exclusion amount (indexed for inflation since 2016) in 2025 of $13,990,000 and the 2025 gift tax annual exclusion of $19,000 (indexed for inflation) for each family member or a beneficiary with an ILIT Crummey withdraw power. The gift tax applicable exclusion amount from the unified credit was added by the 2017 Tax Cut and Jobs Act, which sunsets on December 31, 2025. If Congress does not intervene, the applicable exclusion amount in 2026 will drop to $5,490,000 (indexed for inflation since 2016). Sometimes the gift tax credit amount and especially the annual exclusion are not available if they are dedicated to other uses by the grantor (e.g., annual cash gifts to the family or ILIT beneficiaries). After the credit amount has been used and the exclusions are exceeded, the gift tax kicks in at 40% on the dollar.

2. Use of a GRAT or a CLAT

Under this technique, the ILIT is a remainderman of the grantor retained annuity trust (GRAT) or a charitable lead annuity trust (CLAT). Because of the retained annuity by the grantor or the annuity paid to the charity, the gift is limited to the value of the remainder interest, which can be zeroed out. Thus, a large amount is placed in the GRAT or CLAT with little or no gift. The hope is that the remainder will appreciate in excess of the annuity payment over the term of the GRAT or CLAT, and the grantor will outlive the term of the GRAT, so it will eventually be able to be permanent financing of the ILIT policy premium. A head start can be taken on the appreciation by funding the GRAT or CLAT with discounted assets such as family limited partnership units, subject in the future to the proposed Regulations under Section 2701 and 2704, if and to the extent they become effective. However, all or most of the appreciation is unavailable for ILIT premiums until the GRAT or CLAT term ends.

3. Use of an Installment Sale to a Grantor Trust

Under this technique, the grantor sells assets to the ILIT in return for an installment note charging the AFR (which is either paid currently or accrued). If the assets are properly valued, no gift is involved unless the grantor gives the annual note interest payment to the trust. The hope is that the assets sold will appreciate during the term of the note and/or will produce sufficient income so that the appreciation or income will be able to permanently finance ILIT policy premiums after (sometimes before) the installment note is retired. Again, a head start can be taken on the appreciation by selling discounted assets (e.g., family limited partnership units) to the ILIT, subject in the future to the proposed Regulations under Sections 2701 and 2704, if and to the extent they become effective.

This is where temporary split-dollar premium financing or endorsement economic benefit split-dollar arrangements enter into the equation with the above-described permanent ILIT premium payment techniques.

4. Buying Time

While the outright gifts, a GRAT, a CLAT, or a sale to a grantor trust are creating current or future appreciation within the ILIT, the split-dollar technique allows immediate infusion of premium money to purchase the insurance. As will be discussed later, the gift element of the split-dollar technique is low (at least initially)—the annual AFR for premium financing or the annual term premium for the endorsement economic benefit regime.

5. *Short Term*

Although a split-dollar arrangement can allow the immediate purchase of ILIT insurance contracts with small gift tax consequences, it is a temporary technique. An exit strategy is needed before the interest charges or the term premiums overwhelm the ILIT. If the permanent financing plan works, the appreciation from the three permanent techniques (or a combination of them) will be enough to retire the premium financing promissory note or the employer/donor investment under the endorsement economic benefit split-dollar arrangement and still have funds left over to pay future ILIT premium payments.

III. Some Uses of Leveraged Premium Financing

Premium financing using split-dollar arrangements is very flexible and has many applications. This section briefly discusses the four most common usages of leveraged premium financing using split-dollar arrangements—cross-purchase buy-sell agreements, employee perk of life insurance coverage, informal funding of deferred compensation, and wealth transfer. Some of the following comments (particularly those involving taxes) are discussed in more detail elsewhere in the text of this book.

A. Cross-Purchase Buy-Sell Agreements

Shareholders often enter into a cross-purchase arrangement funded at least partially with life insurance—death proceeds for purchase at death and cash value for lifetime purchases. Each shareholder owns insurance on the other shareholders' lives to finance the arrangement.

1. Reasons for Split-Dollar Arrangements

At least in the early years of the agreement, the corporation is able to assist the shareholders in financing their premium payments, which reduces the cash flow requirements for the shareholders. Loan regime split-dollar is the most advantageous because the corporation's interest in the cash value is limited to the premium loans (plus interest)—excess equity cash value is owned by the shareholder who owns the policy and is available for a life-time buyout. If the economic benefit regime is used, the corporation would own all of the cash value, leaving the shareholder with only the pure death benefit. Furthermore, if the insured is the controlling shareholder, the incidents of ownership of the policy owned by the corporation under the economic benefit regime over the pure death benefit payable to the other shareholders under Treas. Reg. Section 20.2042-1(c)(6) would be attributed to the deceased insured shareholder for estate tax purposes. Another advantage of using split-dollar for cross-purchase buy-sell agreements is that the premium differences among the insured shareholders caused by age or health are shared at the corporate level by all of the shareholders.

The disadvantage of loan regime split-dollar financing is that the corporation's loan is increasing with each premium loan over time, reducing the cash value and death proceeds available to the shareholder for the cross purchase. The corporation could use its funds to redeem part of the stock of the retiring or deceased shareholder. Although all of the policy values would be used in the combined redemption and cross purchase, to the extent the corporation redeems part of the stock, the advantages of a cross purchase are partially lost, such as an increase in stock basis to the surviving shareholders. Thus, in most cases, the cross-purchase split-dollar arrangement is temporary until the shareholder who owns the policy can pay off the loan and shoulder future premium payments. Otherwise, the corporation premium loans will take an increasing part of the policy cash value and death proceeds, and the interest charges paid by the shareholder who owns the policy will become more onerous.

2. *Estate Tax Issue*

If the controlling shareholder is an insured, for estate tax purposes, steps must be taken to avoid the application of incidents of ownership in the part of the death proceeds payable to the non-insured shareholder who owns the policy.[19] For a loan regime split-dollar arrangement, the corporation is merely a creditor and cannot have any incidents of ownership to be attributed to the insured controlling shareholder. However, under either regime, care should be taken if the controlled corporation receives a collateral assignment against the cash value and death proceeds of the policy to secure the repayment to the corporation. The typical collateral assignment would give broad powers to the controlled corporation, which might constitute incidents of ownership in the policy—in case of a default, the controlled corporation would have the ability to withdraw from, surrender, or borrow against the policy. It could be argued that the incidents of ownership are confined to the cash value of the policy and do not taint the death proceeds under the controlling shareholder regulation but that argument would probably not succeed.

However, to play it safe, the collateral assignment should be drafted as restricted access or "bare bones" assignment. The loan agreement and the collateral assignment should prohibit the controlled corporation from exercising any rights under the policy, particularly prohibiting borrowing against the policy, taking any action that would endanger the interest of the non-insured shareholder owner, surrendering the policy, and prohibiting assigning its rights to any owner other than the owning shareholder. In other words, the loan agreement and the collateral assignment restrict the controlled corporation's rights to the receipt of repayment of its loans from the cash value upon surrender by the shareholder owner or from the death proceeds. All other rights in the policy are given to the owning shareholder.

The IRS has blessed restricted bare bones collateral assignments with regard to grandfathered split-dollar arrangements, concluding that the controlled corporation did not possess incidents of ownership to be imputed to the insured controlling shareholder under the assignment.[20]

3. *Other Life Insurance Funding Concerns*

Although not peculiar to split-dollar funding, the use of any life insurance to fund a cross-purchase agreement raises other issues that should be addressed.

a. Multiple Shareholders and Multiple Policies

If there are more than two shareholders participating in the agreement, the number of policies increase geometrically because each shareholder has to own a policy on each other shareholder's life—3 shareholders require 6 policies, 4 shareholders 12 policies, and so on. Note how multiple policies were avoided in identical facts in four 1993 letter rulings[21] in which the shareholders were also partners, and a series of grantor trusts created by the non-insured partners were used to purchase one policy on each life of the insured partner.

b. Transfer for Value

Again, if there are more than two shareholders, and upon the death of one of the shareholders his or her ownership interest in the other surviving shareholders' policies is transferred on a cross-owned basis to the other shareholders, such a transfer would be a transfer for value, with the result that the death proceeds in excess of basis would be ordinary income to the non-insured owner.[22] The arrangement should be structured so that the transfer is to the person who is exempt from the transfer for value rule; the most common exception relied on in these circumstances is a transfer to a partner of the insured. Thus, if the shareholders are also partners in a partnership or members of a limited liability company (LLC) that is taxed as a partnership, the transfer avoids transfer for value.[23]

c. Example

Two brothers each own 50% of the C corporation that operates an active business; none of their respective family members wish to continue to operate the business after the death of either of the shareholders. Accordingly, they have decided to enter into a cross-purchase buy-sell arrangement, fully funded with life insurance on each of their lives, and each policy is owned by the non-insured shareholder. At the first death, the non-insured shareholder will collect the policy proceeds of the insurance on his deceased co-shareholder and will use both proceeds either in whole or in part to purchase the deceased co-shareholder's corporate interest from his successor in interest.

Rather than having each shareholder personally pay the premiums on the policy he owns on his co-shareholder's life, they decide to use loan regime split-dollar arrangement, under which the corporation will lend the premiums due on the policy owned by each shareholder to the shareholder in exchange for a note due at the insured's death, bearing adequate AFR interest. To have the full policy proceeds available to each of the shareholder's at the other's death, the policy is structured with a return of premium rider, which will increase the death benefit by the amount the corporation lends to the policyowner. Using this technique, the shareholders can reduce their personal out-of-pocket costs for acquiring the insurance on their co-shareholder's life to the interest they have to pay the corporation each year rather than having to pay the premiums on the policy they own personally.

B. An Employee Perk of Life Insurance Coverage

An employer can assist an executive in a leveraged purchase of a permanent life insurance policy. The split-dollar arrangement ends at a future date when the employee can assume full premium payments and is able to pay off the employer's loan or purchase the employer's ownership of the policy.

1. Advantages

The employee has insurance coverage at a personal cost (in an employer-pay-all arrangement) of the AFR or term insurance premium, depending whether the loan or economic benefit regime is used, rather than being taxed on the total premium paid by the employer. The arrangement can be structured so that the employer and the executive share the premium payment, which reduces the executive's leverage. Low-cost split-dollar coverage protects against the executive's subsequent loss of insurability. The employer will receive back its premiums plus AFR or its premiums plus any excess cash value, depending whether the loan or economic benefit regime is used. This type of coverage may be useful for key employee retention.

2. *Peculiar Issues*

a. Public Company Split-Dollar Arrangements

Section 402 of the Sarbanes-Oxley Act prohibits personal loans from a public reporting company to directors or executive officers. There is no express guidance for split-dollar arrangements, but most practitioners conclude that loan regime (even if non-recourse) split-dollar arrangements are prohibited. The argument that non-equity economic benefit regime split-dollar arrangements are acceptable is that the IRS does not treat them as loans; however, the guidance under Sarbanes Oxley is provided by the US Securities and Exchange Commission (SEC) and not the IRS. Without SEC guidance, most public reporting companies avoid all split-dollar arrangements for its executive officers after Sarbanes.

b. S Corporation Split-Dollar Arrangements

If there is a split-dollar arrangement between an S corporation and an employee-shareholder, there is some degree of "double taxation" to the shareholder because the S corporation cannot deduct the premium payment from its flow through income and the shareholder also has a taxable economic benefit. This double taxation is diluted to the extent there are other S corporation shareholders without similar split-dollar agreements. As noted later, a split-dollar arrangement even with a sole shareholder may make sense for wealth transfer purposes.

However, the Sixth Circuit concluded that split-dollar economic benefits are not taxed to the S corporation or employee as a distribution of property under the S corporation regulations. The Tax Court and the IRS disagree.[24]

If the shareholder reimburses the S corporation for her or his economic benefit using the economic benefit regime, there will be no preferential dividend creating a second class of stock, which would terminate the S election.[25] However, such reimbursement is income to the S corporation.[26] No such problem exists for the loan regime if interest at least at the AFR is paid by the shareholder.

c. Example

Bill, a young executive, wants life insurance to provide protection for his family in case of his premature death—support of his family, college education for his children, and payment of his home mortgage. Cash flow to pay premiums is a concern. Bill could purchase term insurance to provide the needed coverage. But Bill prefers permanent insurance with cash value that could be accessed during his lifetime for education of his children, supplemental retirement pay, or unforeseen expenses. Plus, the death benefit would be available at his death at an older age without paying rapidly increasing premiums for a term insurance policy.

Bill's employer comes to the rescue, allowing Bill to purchase a permanent insurance policy pursuant to a loan regime split-dollar arrangement with the employer. The employer pays the full premium. Bill pays only the annual AFR and owns all cash value in excess of the employer's aggregate premium loans. As soon as Bill's cash flow sufficiently grows, he can terminate the split-dollar arrangement and pay back his employer, and then he fully owns a permanent insurance policy.

C. Informal Funding of Deferred Compensation

1. Deferred Compensation and Life Insurance

Employers commonly use insurance on an executive's life to informally provide the funds to pay nonqualified deferred compensation to the executive. Death proceeds payable to the employer are received income tax free to provide the funds for death benefit deferred compensation payments, which are deductible. Because of the insurance policy wrap, the cash value buildup is income tax free to the employer until the policy is surrendered or the cash value is accessed by withdrawals in excess of basis to pay lifetime deferred compensation. Policy loans do not result in income to the employer, but interest will accrue on the loans if not paid.

2. How Does the Split-Dollar Arrangement Fit In?

Split-dollar life insurance normally provides a death benefit, but it can also be used to informally back up a deferred compensation plan. If the employer is only looking to the policy cash value to reimburse the employer for the deferred compensation, the employer may enter into a split-dollar agreement with the insured executive so that the executive can benefit from the pure death benefit otherwise unneeded by the employer. This would work very well when the deferred compensation is measured by the cash value of a variable universal life policy when the executive recommends the "deemed" investments of the cash value among various policy mutual funds. In such a case, the cash value equals the deferred compensation. The safer approach to insurance and deferred compensation is not to cross reference the policy and the plan to avoid an IRS assertion of funding. However, when the cash value is the measure of the deferred compensation, reference to the policy in the plan is necessary but an express statement that the reference is solely to determine the amount of deferred compensation and does not give the executive any rights in the policy should answer any funding argument. The employer may want to control the entire cash value for deferred compensation use by using either the economic benefit regime or a non-equity split-dollar arrangement.

3. *Internal Revenue Code Issues*

A vested deferred compensation plan must be an unfunded, unsecured promise to pay in order to avoid immediate income taxation to the executive under Section 83 or the economic benefit doctrine.[27] Informal funding by the employer with assets controlled by the employer and available to the employer's creditors is not "funding" if the executive has no preference to the assets. Employer-owned life insurance can be used as such informal funding.[28] Thus, even though the split-dollar arrangement is with the executive, if the employer's interest in the policy (e.g., cash value) is under its sole control and subject to its creditors, there should be no funding for income tax purposes. Care must be taken in drafting the agreement to keep the informal insurance funding separate from the promised benefit.

4. *ERISA Issues*

To avoid the restrictions of Employee Retirement Income Security Act (ERISA) that would destroy an otherwise nonqualified deferred compensation plan, it must be a so-called "top hat plan," which is unfunded and primarily maintained to provide deferred compensation for a select group of management or highly compensated employees.[29] The rules for "funding" for ERISA are the same as for income tax purposes.[30] Employer-owned life insurance intended to informally fund a top hat deferred compensation or welfare plan is not funding as long as the employer controls the policy, it is subject to the employer's creditors, and the executive is only an unsecured creditor.[31] The informal funding of a deferred compensation agreement with the employer's investment in the cash value of a separate split-dollar life insurance policy does not constitute ERISA funding.[32]

5. *Example*

An employer and executive enter into a deferred compensation agreement that will pay the executive an annual pension equal to 30% of highest annual pay upon retirement at age 65 years. In addition, the employer and executive enter into a separate economic benefit split-dollar agreement whereby the employer owns the policy on the executive's life and endorses to the executive a death benefit equal to five times the executive's annual salary. There is no cross reference between the two agreements. The employer plans to use, but is not required to use, the policy cash value and its share of the death benefit in excess of five times the executive's annual salary to recoup its cost of paying the deferred compensation to the executive and to repay its premium investment plus interest. These facts are similar to those in *Miller v. Heller*. Thus, the executive has a pure death benefit at the cost of a term premium while the employer is informally funding its deferred compensation obligation with a policy that accumulates cash value free of income taxation.

D. Split-Dollar Insurance and Wealth Transfer

1. *Removing a Policy from the Gross Estate and Reducing the Value of Premium Gifts*

A policy is removed from the insured's gross estate if all incidents of ownership are owned by an ILIT or a family member (and the policy was not transferred by the insured within 3 years of death). Unless the ILIT or family member has other assets to pay future premiums, the donor will have to continue annual premium gifts, which may exceed the gift tax annual exclusion and reduce or even eliminate the gift tax exemption.

2. *This Is Where a Split-Dollar Arrangement Is Useful*

If the full premium is paid by the insured or the insured's employer under a split-dollar plan, then the taxable gift to the ILIT each year is the much reduced AFR or the term premium, depending on whether the loan or economic benefit regime is used. If the split-dollar arrangement is between the insured's employer and the ILIT, the economic benefit of the arrangement is treated as two separate transactions—a compensation arrangement between the employer and the insured and a gift arrangement between the insured and the ILIT.[33] A direct split-dollar arrangement between the insured (or a family member) and the ILIT is a private split-dollar arrangement, which could result in an economic benefit taxable gift rather than a full premium gift.[34]

3. *Estate Tax Considerations*

To avoid incidents of ownership in a private split-dollar arrangement, the insured should not own the split-dollar policy. Instead, the ILIT should be the owner with the insured lending the premium under the loan regime or providing the benefit of the economic benefit regime through a non-equity split-dollar arrangement.[35] If the split-dollar arrangement is between the ILIT and a corporation of which the insured is the controlling shareholder, the corporation should not be the owner of the split-dollar policy in order to void attribution of the corporate incidents of ownership over the death proceeds payable to the ILIT under Treas. Reg. Section 20.2042-1(c)(6).[36] The ILIT should be the owner with the corporation lending the premiums under the loan regime or providing the benefit of the economic benefit regime through a non-equity split-dollar arrangement.

The estate tax implications are uncertain for split-dollar arrangements between an ILIT and a partnership of which the insured is a partner. The IRS position is that incidents of ownership for the death proceeds payable to the ILIT are attributed to the insured partner even if he or she is not the controlling partner.[37] There are two ways to avoid this attribution: the partnership agreement expressly prohibits the insured partner from exercising incidents of ownership,[38] or the loan regime is used.

As noted earlier, care is needed where a collateral assignment of the policy to protect the interest of the insured's controlled corporation or partnership in the policy is used. As also noted earlier, a specially drafted restricted or "bare bones" collateral assignment is needed giving all incidents of ownership to the ILIT and reserving to the premium payer only the right to be reimbursed in case of termination of the split-dollar arrangement.

Even though an S corporation split-dollar arrangement may not make sense from an income tax point of view for shareholders with a substantial amount of stock because of double taxation, the arrangement still makes sense for split-dollar policies with an ILIT designed for wealth transfer.[39]

4. *Example*

A settlor creates an ILIT to own a survivorship policy, insuring his life and the life of his wife, with the policy proceeds payable at the second death. The settlor has already used his and his spouse's full gift tax exemptions, and their gift tax annual exclusion gifts are being used for outright gifts to their children and grandchildren.

To allow the trustee of the ILIT to acquire the policy and pay ongoing premiums, the settlor enters into an economic benefit split-dollar arrangement with the ILIT, under which the settlor agrees to advance premiums to the ILIT in exchange for its restricted (or bare bones) receivable, equal to the greater of the premiums advanced or the policy's cash value (disregarding surrender charges). Because of the way the economic benefit cost for survivorship policy is calculated while both insureds are alive, the gift resulting from the arrangement is a minor fraction of the premium advanced, reducing the gift (and potential generation-skipping) tax consequences of the arrangement from the full premium to the small (but ever increasing) economic benefit term cost. As the insureds age, and especially after the first death, the economic benefit term costs may no longer provide transfer tax leverage, at which point the arrangement could be "switched" to a loan regime split-dollar arrangement, under which the gift would be measured by interest rates rather than by economic term costs.

IV. Premium Financing

A. A General Overview of Private or Related Party Premium Financing

Related party loans to pay premiums on a life insurance policy (premium financing) can, in general, take two forms—loans that bear interest at the AFR and those that don't. Loans that at least bear interest at the AFR are generally not governed by Section 7872; those that don't are.

Related party loans that at least bear interest at the AFR can also take two forms—loans that provide for payment of interest on a current (annual) basis and those that accrue interest at the AFR, compound it, and pay it with principal at the end of the term of the loan, each of which has different tax and economic consequences.

Related party loans that don't at least bear interest at the AFR can take three forms—demand loans, term loans, and so-called "hybrid" loans, each of which also has different economic and tax consequences, as also discussed later. These loans, known as interest-free loans—technically, below-market rate loans—are governed by Section 7872, which has the effect of imputing interest at the AFR for both income and transfer tax purposes.

For interest-free *demand* loans, the interest is imputed for tax purposes on an annual basis, at the short-term AFR (which changes monthly but can be averaged annually). For interest-free *term* loans, the interest is imputed at the short-term, mid-term, or long-term AFR (depending on the term of the loan) and is fixed for the term of the loan, but all of the interest over the expected term of the loan, discounted back to present value, is imputed in the year of the loan.

Interest-free *hybrid* loans have characteristics of both demand and term loans. Gift term loans are one form of hybrid loans; they are treated, for purposes of imputing interest *for income tax, but not for transfer tax purposes*, as demand loans, but the AFR is fixed and is determined based on the stated term of the loan. Because this exception doesn't apply for transfer tax purposes, gift term loans are treated as term loans for transfer tax purposes, with the negative transfer tax consequences already described.

Under the *still proposed* Section 7872 regulations, applicable to interest-free loans in general (having nothing to do with premium financing arrangements) and to pre-Final Split-Dollar Regulation arrangements, *only* compensation term loans that terminate with employment are treated as hybrid loans; loans based on life expectancy are, under these proposed Regulations, treated as term loans.

However, under the *Final* Split-Dollar Section 7872 Regulations (which, as noted later, will apply to premium financing arrangements entered into or materially modified after the effective date of the Regulations), *both* compensation term loans that terminate with employment *and* term loans in which the term is determined by life expectancy (those payable at the death of an insured) are treated as hybrid loans. For hybrid loans payable at the death of an insured, if the insured outlives her or his life expectancy under the IRS tables, the loan converts to a demand loan thereafter, with the transfer tax consequences note earlier.

As a practical matter, these rules will mean, in most cases, that the only interest-free loans that will be practical are demand loans, in which the interest rate changes every year; interest-free gift term loans will not make sense from a transfer tax point of view because of the bunching of the discounted present value of the imputed interest over the expected term of the loan into the initial year of the loan. Interest-bearing term loans (with interest paid or accrued at the AFR) will make sense, including those that are in excess of the current year premium, to lock in today's rate for the term of the loan.

Note, however, the impact of the provisions of the Final Split-Dollar Regulations if the lender and the borrower are related and the lender is "to pay" the interest amount to the borrower; if the interest is waived, cancelled, or forgiven; or if the arrangement is non-recourse (an undefined term in the Regulations).

B. The Possible Application of Federal Reserve Regulation U to Loans Used to Acquire Variable Policies

In cases involving very large premium loans—defined as $200,000 of credit extended in a calendar quarter or $500,000 outstanding at any one time—which are secured by the policy, if the policy being financed is a variable policy, the loans will be considered loans to purchase margin stock that is secured, directly or indirectly, by margin stock (the underlying securities in the separate accounts) and will require compliance with Regulation U of the Board of Governors of the Federal Reserve System. According to the Board's Staff, the policy itself isn't margin stock; only the underlying funds are.

The staff of the Federal Reserve Board has concluded that a loan to acquire a variable policy by a lender, other than the insurer, is indirectly secured by margin stock, at least where the policy is pledged as collateral. A loan by the insurer against the policy would not be because while that loan is outstanding, the separate accounts do not participate in the performance of the underlying investments.[40]

A loan used to purchase or carry a variable policy but not secured by the policy would not be considered to be directly or indirectly secured by the policy (unless the policy accounted for a significant portion of the assets of the borrower in violation of the safe harbor rule). If the lender, in good faith, has not relied on the margin stock as collateral in extending the credit, the arrangement is not a margin loan.[41]

Importantly, as noted earlier, to be considered a "lender" for this purpose, the lender would have to extend credit of $200,000 or more for such purpose in any calendar quarter or have $500,000 or more in margin credit outstanding.[42]

Under Regulation U, the amount of any such loan treated as a margin loan will be limited to 50% of the value (at the date of the transaction) of the margin stock securing the loan.[43]

The lender, if not a broker or bank, may have to register with the Federal Reserve if the loan meets the threshold dollar amount test, described earlier (unless the loan is outside the "ordinary course of business," which is interpreted as an extremely narrow exception).

C. Exit Strategies

Like split-dollar arrangements, premium financing arrangements should be planned at the outset with an exit strategy for terminating the arrangement during the insured's lifetime. Because each year's premium is treated as a separate loan, the loans and interest accumulate over the insured's lifetime. This is especially an issue for loans with interest accrued, rather than paid or imputed, because the interest is compounded.

These are, by definition, "equity arrangements" because policy values in excess of amounts due the lender could eventually be used to do a lifetime termination, without tax consequences, unlike post-Final Split-Dollar Regulation arrangements taxed under the economic benefit regime, which will always be done as "non-equity" arrangements, with the entire cash value returned to the premium provider.

For trust-owned policies using premium financing, leveraged gifts to the trust (of discounted entities subject to the proposed Sections 2701 and 2704 Regulations) or non-gift transfers of growth assets or entities (installment sales, other loans unrelated to the policy, zeroed-out grantor retained annuity trusts [if the trust isn't a generation-skipping trust], zeroed-out charitable lead trusts, as examples) should be considered to create a side fund that could be used, either alone or with policy values, to exit the arrangement during the insured's life. In most of these strategies, grantor trust status for the trust would normally be advantageous (and is required for an effective installment sale).

An additional upfront loan from the grantor, with interest paid or accrued at the AFR, would create an immediate side fund, which could be used to pay interest or exit the transaction (if the trust could earn more than the AFR charged on this loan). This might be particularly attractive in an era of low interest rates to lock in the rate for the term of the loan. Because this loan would be unrelated to the policy, it presumably would be a gift term loan and, for the reasons noted earlier, would not be structured as an interest-free loan.

In any event, consideration should be given to designing the policy so that the death benefit increases to track the premium loans (and accrued interest) to keep the trust's death benefit level usually done through the use of a policy rider, at the cost of extra premiums.

Creating a side fund would allow termination of the loan during the insured's lifetime, avoiding the potential tax issue raised by termination of the trust's grantor trust status at the grantor's death while the loan is outstanding, ending either the gifting needed to service the loan in current interest payment transactions or the erosion of the death benefit in interest accrual transactions, ending an increasingly expensive arrangement that reduces the death benefit left in the trust, and avoiding issues under the "to pay" provision of the regulations, discussed earlier.

However, it could increase the potential tax issue on termination of the trust's grantor status at the grantor's death, as discussed later, because the trust will have more assets, which could then be treated as sold by the grantor to the trust in exchange for the outstanding loan.

D. Premium Financing Formats

The legal and tax consequences of these transactions depend on the identity of the lender, the relationship between the lender and the borrower, and the terms of the loan; each format has different tax and economic consequences.

Private premium financing generally involves interest-bearing loans to an ILIT to pay premiums, by the insured(s), an employer, a family entity (e.g., an LLC), or another family member, with stated interest at the AFR, paid annually or accrued, principal repaid at death. This is an alternative to private split-dollar arrangement with a different measure of the tax consequences.

If interest is to be paid annually, the gift would be the amount needed to be gifted each year by the lender to pay the interest to the insured (if the trust has no other assets) rather than economic benefit amounts. If the trust has been previously funded, it could pay the interest without gifts from the insured lender. If the trust has no other funding, when the policy has sufficient cash value, the trustee could withdraw from or borrow against the policy to pay the interest, also avoiding ongoing gifts by the insured lender.

Any such transaction would have to have real world economic consequences, to be respected for tax purposes; the trust would want to avoid borrowing or withdrawing the amount of the interest at the same time it is to be paid to the insured(s). If the policy were a modified endowment contract (MEC), the loan or withdrawal could have tax consequences to the trust (or to the grantor if the trust were a grantor trust).

If the interest is to be accrued, compounded, and paid at the death of the insured (or survivor of the insureds), there would be no gifting required to allow the trust to pay interest to the insured lender (if the trust wasn't otherwise funded); this is sometimes called "giftless premium financing."

Under the Final Split-Dollar Regulations, under a facts and circumstances test, if the interest is "to be paid by" the lender, the arrangement will be treated as a split-dollar loan subject to Section 7872. To avoid this rule, there needs to be a disconnect between the lender's gifts to the trust and its payment of interest to the lender, which is a matter of degree, with no bright line test available.

The insured, as premium provider, won't have an interest in policy values in excess of the loan amount. The trust will own cash values that exceed the loan, plus interest, but there will be no "equity" issue for gift tax purposes, as there would be in a private endorsement split-dollar arrangement. This will limit the amount includible in the insured's estate to the premiums advanced (plus interest received or accrued over the term of the loan) and leave all excess policy values in the trust, with no tax consequences.

There is an estate tax issue for the insured raised by this arrangement under Section 2042(2) if the policy is used as security for the loans. Accordingly, the assignment to the insured must be "restricted," as in a controlling shareholder or private split-dollar arrangement,[44] or the arrangement would have to be "unsecured," with the policy not used as security for the loan.

The loan itself (ignoring the security issue, described earlier) will not create an incident of ownership under Section 2042(2). See Ltr. Rul. 9809032, holding that an insured's loans to the trust to pay premiums did not, in and of themselves, create an incident of ownership. In any event, the value of the note would be includable in the insured's estate under Section 2031, including all accrued interest.

If the policy is a survivorship policy and only one of the insureds lends premium amounts to the trust, if he or she dies first, the note will be includible in his or her estate, and consideration must be given to its disposition at death. The note could be bequeathed to the surviving spouse or insured in a way that qualifies for the estate tax marital deduction; because the original lender was an insured, any security interest for the loan would have had to have been restricted from inception, but if it weren't, adding the restrictions then would begin a 3-year rule under Section 2035. Alternatively, the note could be bequeathed to the trust, where it would be cancelled by operation of law (because the trust would own its own note), without tax consequences under Section 102 because it was acquired by bequest.

If the lender is the employer of the insured (or one of the insureds), the loan will have federal income tax consequences, and care will have to be taken to comply with the requirements of Section 409A, as discussed later.

E. The Final Split-Dollar Regulations

Section 1.61-22(b) of the Final Split-Dollar Regulations defines a split-dollar arrangement as one between an "owner" and a "non-owner" of a life insurance contract, pursuant to which either party pays all (or a part) of the premiums and at least one party is entitled to recover all or a portion of the premiums and that recovery is to be made from or is secured by the proceeds of a policy. The taxation of a split-dollar arrangement under the Final Split-Dollar Regulations is divided into two distinct regimes—the economic benefit regime and the loan regime. The key to which regime will apply is identifying the owner and non-owner of the policy.

The economic benefit regime applies in a donor–donee split-dollar arrangement if the donor is also the owner (or is treated as the owner) of the life insurance contract. The loan regime applies in a donor–donee split-dollar arrangement if the donee is the owner of the life insurance contract. The person named as the policy owner generally is the owner for purposes of these rules. However, a donor is treated as the owner of a life insurance contract under an economic benefit split-dollar arrangement between the donor and a donee if the only economic benefit that will be provided under the arrangement is current life insurance protection.[45]

The Final Split-Dollar Regulations provide that a payment made pursuant to a split-dollar life insurance arrangement is treated as a loan for federal tax purposes, and the owner and non-owner are treated as the borrower and the lender, respectively, if (1) the payment is made either directly or indirectly by the non-owner to the owner (including a premium payment made by the non-owner directly or indirectly to the insurance company with respect to the policy held by the owner); (2) the payment is a loan under general principles of federal tax law or, if it is not a loan under general principles of federal tax law, a reasonable person nevertheless would expect the payment to be repaid in full to the non-owner (whether with or without interest); and (3) the repayment is to be made from, or is secured by, the policy's death benefit proceeds, the policy's cash surrender value, or both.[46]

Loans used by the borrower to pay premiums on a policy ("private premium financing arrangements") are generally included in the definition of split-dollar loan, although in most cases, as long as "sufficient interest" is paid (or accrued), the general tax rules governing loans and not the special split-dollar loan rules of the Final Split-Dollar Regulations will apply. To determine whether interest is sufficient, the Final Split-Dollar Regulations divide loans into two categories: (1) demand loans, payable in full on the demand of the lender, or (2) term loans, payable on a specific date. For purposes of these rules, as discussed earlier, a loan payable on the death of the insured is considered a hybrid loan, with characteristics of both types of loans.[47]

A split-dollar term loan is tested on the day the loan is made to determine if the loan provides for sufficient interest. A split-dollar term loan provides for sufficient interest if the imputed loan amount equals or exceeds the amount loaned. The imputed loan amount is the present value of all payments due under the loan, determined as of the date the loan is made, using a discount rate equal to the AFR in effect on that date. The AFR used must be appropriate for the loan's term (short term, midterm, or long term) and for the compounding period used in computing the present value. The term of a split-dollar loan payable on the death of an individual (including the death of the last survivor of a group of individuals) is the individual's actuarial life expectancy, determined using the tables under Section 72 on the day the loan is made.[48] Such a loan that provides for sufficient interest is not subject to the imputed interest rules of Section 7872, but it is subject to the original issue discount (OID) rules.[49]

However, as described later, there are special rules for these loans even when interest is paid or accrued at the AFR, namely, (1) if the loan is "non-recourse"; (2) if the lender is "to pay" the interest to the borrower; (3) if interest is waived, cancelled, or forgiven; and (4) there are special loan repayment ordering rules. There are also special rules under the Final Split-Dollar Regulations applicable to loans that provide for variable interest rates or one or more contingent payments, which should not apply to typical private premium financing arrangements. Those special rules of the Final Split-Dollar Regulations applicable to premium financing are:

1. Non-recourse Loans

If a payment made under a split-dollar loan is "non-recourse," the Final Split-Dollar Regulations treat the loan as a loan that provides for contingent payments, increasing the complexity of calculating the tax consequences and testing for the adequacy of interest.[50] The word "non-recourse" is not defined in the Final Split-Dollar Regulations; therefore, it isn't clear if it is broad enough to include a recourse loan to a trust with no assets other than a policy or a loan to such a trust when the policy is not taken back as collateral.[51]

The Final Split-Dollar Regulations contain an exception, providing that this general rule will not apply with respect to a split-dollar loan that is non-recourse if the parties to the arrangement provide a written representation with respect to the loan that indicates that a "reasonable person" would expect all payments under the loan to be made.[52] The Final Split-Dollar Regulations require that, subject to future IRS rules, the representation regarding expectation of payment be attached to the federal income tax returns of both parties, for each year such a loan is made under the arrangement.

Because it is difficult to determine whether a loan to an insurance trust that has no other assets is or is not non-recourse, this written representation requirement should be complied with, to avoid treating the loan as one that provides for contingent payments. Finally, as discussed later, filing the representation provides additional support for the proposition that the loan will be respected for federal tax purposes and will avoid the imposition of a deferral charge, described later, if any interest due is waived, cancelled, or forgiven.

2. *Interest to Be Paid by the Lender*

The Final Split-Dollar Regulations provide that stated interest to be paid currently on a loan will be disregarded (converting it to a loan governed by Section 7872), if "all or a portion of the interest is to be paid directly or indirectly by the lender or a person related to the lender."[53] A "facts and circumstances" test is used to determine if the interest is "to be paid" by the lender; there is no definition in the Final Split-Dollar Regulations of the phrase "to be paid."[54]

In addition, although not described in these examples, in a donor–donee arrangement, if the facts and circumstances show that the donor is "to pay" the interest to the donee (as a gift), as is common in donor–donee premium financing arrangements, in which interest is to be paid currently, the loan would become subject to Section 7872.

It is unclear how a less formal arrangement might be treated, such as one in which a donor makes occasional gifts to the donee of the interest due or one or more larger gifts that are unrelated to the interest due (but that are invested and used, over the years, to pay the interest).

3. *Waiver, Cancellation, or Forgiveness of Interest*

The Final Split-Dollar Regulations provide that if accrued but unpaid interest on a split-dollar loan is later waived, cancelled, or forgiven by the lender, then the waiver, cancellation, or forgiveness is treated under the loan regime as if, on that date, the interest had in fact been paid to the lender by the borrower and retransferred by the lender to the borrower.[55] Accordingly, even split-dollar loans that state adequate interest are still subject to the Final Split-Dollar Regulations if unpaid interest is waived, cancelled, or forgiven by the lender.[56]

In addition, the amount deemed transferred and retransferred is increased by a deferral charge equal to three percentage points over the underpayment of tax interest penalty. The deferral charge is designed to recoup the time-value-of-money loss that is suffered by the reduction or elimination of non-loan payments that resulted from the subsequently waived stated interest. However, if the parties to a split-dollar life insurance arrangement make the representation as described regarding the expectation of payment of the note and the interest actually paid is less than the interest required to be accrued on the split-dollar loan, the excess of the interest required to be accrued over the interest actually paid is treated as waived, cancelled, or forgiven by the lender but is not subject to the deferral charge.

The purpose of this rule is to ensure that the parties to a split-dollar loan ultimately recognize interest at least equal to the AFR. The character of the non-loan payment depends on the relationship of the parties; the payment is compensation if the split-dollar loan is in connection with the performance of services and the lender is the employer, is a Section 301 distribution or capital contribution, if the parties are a corporation and a shareholder, or a gift if they are, as here, donor and donee.

4. *Loan Repayment Rules*

Finally, under the Final Split-Dollar Regulations, it is not possible for the parties to choose which of the series of premium financing loans is to be repaid first (e.g., those loans that bear the highest interest rates). Instead, under Regulation Section 1.7872-15(k), repayment of split-dollar loans must be paid first as unpaid interest and then principal, both in the order the loans were made.

5. *Summary of Premium Financing Formats*

To summarize the transfer tax effects of each of the potential loan arrangements:

(a) A loan with interest paid annually, at the AFR, would require a gift by the donor to the trust to allow the trust to pay the interest due each year (subject to the "to pay" provisions of the Regulations, described earlier) unless the trust was otherwise funded. At the insured's death, the principal of the note would be includible in his or her estate, as would all of the unspent interest received during the term of the note.

(b) For a loan that accrued interest at the AFR, compounded, and added it to principal, there would be no gift for transfer tax purposes. At the insured's death, his or her estate would include the principal amount of the note, increased by all of the accrued interest.

(c) A non–interest-bearing demand loan would increase the interest rate risk but would only include the principal of the loan, not any interest, in the lender's estate for estate tax purposes.

(d) Finally, an interest-bearing loan requiring interest to be paid annually, in which the interest is forgiven annually, would only include the loan principal in the insured's estate, but the representation described earlier must be filed each year with the parties' federal income tax returns each year a loan is made under the arrangement to avoid the deferral charge on the gift of the interest.

F. Federal Income Taxation of the Grantor and the Trust

When the lender is the insured settlor of the trust that owns the policy, the way in which the trust, the grantor of the trust, and the beneficiaries of the trust are taxed for federal income tax purposes depends on whether the trust (or a portion of the trust) is classified for income tax purposes as a "grantor trust" or a "non-grantor trust."

If the settlor is treated as the owner of all or a portion of a trust (i.e., the trust is a grantor trust), the settlor must include in his or her personal income tax computation all items of income, deductions, and credits against tax attributable to the portion of the trust for which the individual is deemed to be the owner.[57] If a settlor is deemed to be the owner of the entire trust, all income, deductions, and credits generated by the trust flow through to the settlor.

The regulations under Section 671[58] define a "grantor" as including "any person to the extent such person creates a trust, or directly or indirectly makes a gratuitous transfer of property to a trust." However, the regulations state that a person who creates a trust but makes no gratuitous transfers to the trust may be a grantor of the trust but is not treated as an owner of any portion of the trust under Sections 671 through 677 or 679. Accordingly, to create a grantor trust within the meaning of these rules, the person who wishes to be treated as the owner of such trust for income tax purposes must make a gratuitous transfer to the trust. The regulations do not set forth a de minimus amount that is required for the transfer to qualify as a gratuitous transfer.

If all or a portion of a trust is not treated as a grantor trust because the grantor is not treated as owning all or a portion of the trust, the trust, or that portion of the trust, is taxed as a non-grantor trust. Non-grantor trusts, unlike grantor trusts, are treated as separate taxable entities for income tax purposes. The income earned by a non-grantor trust is allocated between the trust itself and the beneficiaries of the trust by allowing the trust to deduct some amounts paid to the beneficiaries.[59] A non-grantor trust is generally allowed to deduct the amount of distributable net income (DNI)[60] that is distributed to a beneficiary during each year.[61] The beneficiary who receives the DNI is required to include the amount of income received during the taxable year.[62]

1. Federal Income Taxation of the Trust

a. The Grantor Trust Rules

A trust, or a portion of a trust, is treated as a grantor trust for income tax purposes if the grantor retains certain powers over or interests in the trust. In general, the grantor of a trust will be treated as the owner of all or a portion of a trust if (1) the grantor holds a reversionary interest in a portion of the trust and, if the value of the reversionary interest on the date that the trust created is more than 5% of the value of the total trust;[63] (2) the grantor or a non-adverse party (or both) has the power to dispose of the beneficial enjoyment of either corpus or income, exercisable without an adverse party's approval or consent;[64] (3) certain powers are exercisable primarily for the grantor's benefit rather than for that of the trust beneficiaries;[65] (4) the grantor or a non-adverse party has the power to revoke the trust,[66] (5) the grantor (or his or her spouse) has the right to income from the trust; or (6) importantly for insurance trusts, if trust income must be (or, in the discretion of the grantor or a non-adverse party, can be) applied to the payment of premiums on policies of insurance on the life of the grantor or the grantor's spouse.[67]

Under Section 672(a), an adverse party is a person having a substantial beneficial interest in the trust that would be adversely affected by the exercise or non-exercise of a power (i.e., a trust beneficiary); a non-adverse party is any other person.

b. The Ubiquitous Section 677(a)(3) Grantor Trust Power and Its Arguably More Reliable and More Flexible Alternatives

There are several powers that could be included in an insurance trust that would make the trust a grantor trust for income tax purposes but that would not cause the policy proceeds to be included in the grantor's gross estate for estate tax purposes—that is, powers that are income tax sensitive but not estate tax sensitive. The most common power used for this purpose is the requirement or the trustee's discretionary power (not requiring the consent of an adverse party) to pay premiums on insurance policies on the life of the grantor or her or his spouse out of trust income.

Under Section 677(a)(3), the grantor of a trust is treated as the owner of any trust (or a portion of any trust) as to which (1) the grantor or a non-adverse party may apply trust income to the payment of premiums on policies of insurance on the life of the grantor or the grantor's spouse or (2) trust income must be so applied.[68] Such a trust should be a grantor trust (and the grantor should be taxed on all of the income of the trust) even if trust income is not actually used to pay premiums on a policy on the grantor's life as long as the trust has income and owns such a policy.[69]

A literal reading of Section 677(a)(3) would indicate that in any case in which all of the trust income must or could be used to pay premiums on a policy on the grantor's life, all items relating to the trust's income should be deemed to be owned by the grantor for income tax purposes regardless of whether the income is actually used for that purpose. When both income and principal could be used for the payment of premiums and when unused income is added to principal, it would likewise seem that the items relating to income deemed owned by the grantor for income tax purposes would include both items relating to ordinary income and items relating to corpus.

Although trust provisions preventing trust income from being used to pay insurance premiums would seem to make Section 677(a)(3) inapplicable to such an insurance trust, reaching this conclusion is not as simple as it might seem. There is very little authority on this issue, and much of the authority that does exist is based on the predecessor to Section 677(a)(3).[70] The lack of authority is no doubt in large part attributable to the fact that the IRS Service (hereinafter, the Service) is currently, and has for some time been, refusing to issue private letter rulings regarding the status of ILITs when the trustee has the power to use trust income or principal to pay premiums on policies insuring the grantor's life.[71] Finally, most of the letter rulings relating to Section 677[72] have focused not on whether the trust would be a grantor trust or a non-grantor trust but instead have focused on whether the entire trust or only a part of the trust will be treated as owned by the grantor for income tax purposes under Section 677(a)(3).[73]

Ltr. Rul. 8839008, however, is instructive on the issue of whether an insurance trust can ever be treated as a non-grantor trust. There, grantors, husband and wife, created two irrevocable trusts that did not, at that time, own, nor pay premiums on, any life insurance policies on the life of either grantor. The trust instruments provided that "Trust income shall not be applied toward the payment of insurance premiums for policies on the life of any contributor to Trust." Furthermore, any undistributed income was to be accumulated and added to corpus. Several years later, each trust purchased a survivorship policy on the lives of the grantors, paying the single premium out of the trust principal. The amount of the premium exceeded each trust's total taxable income for that year. In ruling on whether these trusts were grantor trusts under Section 677(a)(3), the Service began by drawing a distinction between trust accounting income and income as determined for tax purposes.

The Service concluded that the trust instrument prevented only the use of trust accounting income from being used to pay premiums but that the source of premium payments for trust accounting purposes is immaterial for purposes of Section 677(a)(3).[74] Therefore, because the amount paid for the insurance premium exceeded the taxable income of each trust during the year the policies were purchased, the grantors were treated as owners of the entire taxable income of the trusts for that year.

Although Ltr. Rul. 8839008 suggests that it would be difficult for an insurance trust to be treated as a non-grantor trust under Section 677(a)(3), it could be argued that the Service went too far in reaching its conclusion with regard to the meaning of the term "income" in Section 677(a)(3). To begin with, the regulation relied on by the Service in Ltr. Rul. 8839008 specifically limits the applicability of the definition of "income" to mean "taxable income" as defined in the Regulations; it does not purport to define "income" as it is used in the Code, a point that the Service glosses over in this ruling. In addition, in the ruling the Service uses "income" to mean "accounting income" for purposes of Section 677(a)(3), but it does not give the term the same meaning as it is used in the trust instrument in question. On the facts of the ruling, there is no indication that by using the word "income" in its restriction on the source of premium payments, the grantor intended to mean "accounting income" rather than "taxable income."

Furthermore, if Congress, in enacting Section 677(a)(3), had intended for the source of premium payments to be immaterial, it could have written Section 677(a) to apply to both trust income and corpus rather than just income, as it did in Sections 673 through 675.[75] The Service's argument under Section 677(a)(3) in the letter ruling is also less than compelling because of the treatment specifically given to payments of trust corpus distributed to fulfill the grantor's legal obligations of support under Section 677(b). Section 677(b) states that to the extent that the grantor's legal obligation of support is "paid out of corpus or out of other than income for the taxable year," such amounts will be taxed to the grantor under Section 662 and not under the grantor trust provisions. The fact that Congress felt compelled to expressly address the use of principal and non-taxable income with regard to distributions that fulfill the grantor's legal obligation of support under Section 677(b) implies that it did not intend the same result under Section 677(a)(3), where the statute is silent as to the treatment of principal. Had Congress meant for principal to be treated under Section 677(a)(3) as the Service suggests in Ltr. Rul. 8839008, it could have so provided.

Through the taxable income–accounting income distinction raised in Ltr. Rul. 8839008, the Service is attempting to broaden the reach of Section 677(a)(3) beyond the meaning generally ascribed to the section and its predecessors by the courts.[76] The courts have generally restricted attempts by the Service to expand the predecessors of Section 677(a)(3). Although most of the cases interpreting the predecessor to Section 677(a)(3) date from the 1930s and 1940s, they are helpful in interpreting Section 677(a)(3) because of the relatively minor differences between Section 677(a)(3) and its predecessors.[77]

The interaction of three variables determined the results in the case law under the predecessors of Section 677(a)(3). The three variables were (1) the ability of the trustee to use trust income to pay premiums, (2) whether the trust held an insurance policy on the life of the grantor,[78] and (3) whether the trustee actually paid premiums on such an insurance policy out of the income of the trust.

The easiest situations to resolve were those when (1) the trustee was not prohibited from using trust income to pay premiums, the trust owned an insurance policy on the grantor's life, and the trustee paid premiums on that policy out of the trust income[79] and (2) the trustee was prohibited from using trust income to pay premiums, the trust did not own an insurance policy on the grantor's life, and the trustee did not pay premiums on that policy out of the trust income.[80] These two situations fall directly inside or outside, respectively, of the scope the predecessor of Section 677(a)(3).

If a trust were to allow the trustee to pay premiums on and were to hold an insurance policy on the grantor's life but not pay premiums on it out of the trust income, then under the holding of *Chandler v. Comm'r*,[81] the trust would not be a grantor trust under Section 167(a)(3). There, the trust instrument provided that premiums should be paid out of trust income only to the extent not paid by insurance policy dividends and contributions from the grantor. If the income had been used to pay the premiums on the insurance policy held by the trust, that income would have been taxable to the grantor, but because no income was used to pay the premiums, the court held that Section 167(a)(3) did not apply.

Likewise, a trust that granted the trustee the ability to pay premiums but which neither held an insurance policy on the grantor's life nor used its income to pay premiums will not be considered a grantor trust under Section 167(a)(3). This situation arose in both *Moore v. Comm'r*[82] and *Weil v. Comm'r*,[83] in which the Service attempted to extend the application of Section 167(a)(3) to trusts that simply allowed for trustees to pay premiums on insurance policies regardless of whether the trusts actually held insurance policies or paid any premiums. In *Moore*, the trust instrument provided that the trustee "may invest in and/or pay the premiums on policies." In *Weil*, the trust provided that the net income of the trust property should be used to pay the premiums on policies. In neither case did the trusts hold insurance policies or pay premiums.

In both instances, the Service argued that the trust income was taxable to the grantor under Section 167(a)(3) merely because the trust income could be used to pay premiums. In ruling against the Service's broad reading of Section 167(a)(3), the courts noted that the application of Section 167(a)(3) depended on the existence in the tax year of policies that it would have been physically possible for the trustees to pay premiums and then only to the extent of the amount of premiums so payable. The courts held that in the absence of an insurance policy and premiums paid out of the income of the trust, Section 167(a)(3) could not be used to treat the trusts as grantor trusts.

In *Rand v. Comm'r*,[84] the court considered the situation where the trust owned an insurance policy and the trustees paid premiums on the policy out of trust income even though the trust did not specifically allow for the payment of premiums out of income. The taxpayer argued that although nothing under state law prohibited a trustee from investing in life insurance and the trust was silent on this issue, the use of trust income to pay insurance policy premiums was not authorized by the trust instrument and was therefore a breach of trust. The court found this result inconceivable, noting that the taxpayer was both grantor and trustee and that it was unlikely that the taxpayer, as trustee, would administer the trust against the wishes of the taxpayer, as grantor. The court concluded that even when a trust was silent as to whether income could be used to pay premiums, Section 167(a)(3) dictated grantor trust status for a trust that held an insurance policy on the grantor's life, the income of which was used to pay premiums.[85]

Finally, there is a question as to how a trust will be treated under Section 677(a)(3) if it owns an insurance policy on the grantor's life, the trustees are specifically prohibited from paying premiums out of trust income, and no such premium payments are made out of the trust income.[86] As discussed earlier, *Chandler*,[87] *Moore*,[88] and *Weil*[89] can all be read to stand for the proposition that a trust is a grantor trust only to the extent that trust income is used to pay premiums on an insurance policy on the life of the grantor. In addition, *Rand*[90] indicates that whether a trust expressly provides the trustee with the power to pay premiums out of trust income is immaterial. The court in *Rand* also seemed to imply that even if the trust specifically prohibited the use of income for the payment of premiums, the breach of trust by the trustee who uses trust income to pay premiums would not prevent grantor trust treatment for the trust under Section 167(a)(3).

All of these cases, along with a number of other old cases decided under Section 167(a)(3),[91] seem to suggest that the most important variable to be considered when determining whether a trust will be considered a grantor trust under Section 677(a)(3) is whether trust income is actually used to pay premiums on a policy on the life of the grantor (or the grantor's spouse). Accordingly, although there is no authority clearly stating that an ILIT specifically prohibiting the use of income to pay premiums and that either has no income or that never used its income to pay premiums will be considered a non-grantor trust, it seems that under the case law applying the predecessor to Section 677(a)(3), such a trust would not be considered a grantor trust.

Accordingly, the older case law applying Section 167(a)(3) is in conflict with the Service's position in Ltr. Rul. 8839008. Although in the ruling, the Service tried to eliminate the distinction between principal and income under Section 677(a)(3) by creating a "trust accounting income" and "taxable income" dichotomy, the general weight of the prior case law is that the trust must own an insurance policy on the life of the grantor, and the premiums on that policy must be paid out of the trust *income* during the taxable year for the trust to be considered a grantor trust. The assertion that it is immaterial whether the payments were actually made out of income or principal as long as the amount of the payments exceeded the taxable income of the trust, is an excessively broad reading of Section 677(a)(3) in light of the substantial precedents under the predecessor to Section 677(a)(3) holding to the contrary, as well as a literal reading of the statute.

Therefore, it seems that a life insurance trust will not *automatically* be considered a grantor trust under Section 677(a)(3) merely because it contains a provision that has become boilerplate requiring or allowing the trustee to use income to pay premiums on the trust's policy on the life of the insured (or his or her spouse), without the consent or approval of an adverse party. Although the trust may provide for the payment of premiums out of trust income and may hold an insurance policy on the life of the grantor or his or her spouse, as long as no trust income is actually used to pay premiums on that policy, because, for instance, it is an otherwise unfunded trust, which has no income, the trust should not be considered a grantor trust.[92] Although an express prohibition mandating that the trustees not use income to pay premiums could act as a safeguard against grantor trust status for the trust, the trust will only be treated as a non-grantor trust to the extent that the trustee actually complies with the trust instrument and does not use trust income to pay premiums.

Possible ways to ensure that an ILIT will be a non-grantor trust, despite Section 677(a)(3), are for the trust to be drafted so that either income is automatically distributed to the beneficiaries upon receipt or so that income is segregated in a separate accrued income account that cannot, under the terms of the trust, be used to pay premiums on policies on the grantor's life (or his or her spouse). In either situation, premium payments for policies on the grantor's life could not be paid out of income, barring a breach of trust; thus, the trust should be a non-grantor trust unless such a breach were to occur. To the extent that Ltr. Rul. 8839008 is correct with regard to its "taxable income" versus "trust accounting income" dichotomy, any prohibition on the use of trust income or any automatic distribution of trust income should be drafted in such a way that the income to which the prohibition or distribution applies is the "taxable income" of the trust.

Perhaps the best way to ensure that an insurance trust won't be treated as a grantor trust under Section 677(a)(3) is to require that any discretionary use of trust income to pay premiums on a policy on the life of the grantor or his or her spouse be consented to by an "adverse party"[93]—a trust beneficiary whose interest would be affected by such a use of trust income.[94]

A related issue is raised by Howard Zaritsky and Steven Leimberg, in *Tax Planning with Life Insurance*. They note in section 5.03[3][ii] that "one of the most difficult aspects of this subsection [677(a)(3)] is determining what portion of a trust is owned by a grantor on account of such possible [premium] payments." As they discuss, there is a line of old cases, dating from the 1930s and 1940s, supporting the position that only items of trust income relating to premium payments actually made should be deemed owned by the grantor under what is now Section 677(a)(3).[95]

Given the lack of clear authority on this issue, a taxpayer would probably be justified in taking either position, that is, that he or she is the deemed owner of all items relating to the trust's income, deductions, or credits or, alternatively, that he or she is deemed the owner of only a portion of those items relating to premiums actually paid out of trust income on policies insuring his or her life (or the life of his or her spouse). As noted in *Tax Planning with Life Insurance*, however, the language of Section 677(a)(3) seems to indicate that as long as all of the income *could* be used to pay premiums on policies on the grantor's life, the grantor should be deemed the owner of the entire trust for income tax purposes.

Accordingly, if it is important to be sure the entire trust will be treated as a grantor trust for income tax purposes, not relying on the Section 677(a)(3) power *(and in fact specifically negating it)* may make sense. In these trusts, adding an additional grantor trust power, which would not be estate tax sensitive, should be considered—and, for the reasons discussed later, the Section 677(a)(3) power should actually be affirmatively negated.

One such power is the administrative power to reacquire trust assets by substituting assets having an equivalent fair market value, held in a nonfiduciary power (by the grantor or by any other—presumably—non-adverse person),[96] see *Jordahl v. CIR*,[97] which held that such a power held by the grantor-insured was not an incident of ownership in the policy owned by the trust for purposes of Section 2042(2). In *Jordahl*, however, this power was held in a *fiduciary capacity*; query if the estate tax result would have been the same for a power held in a non-fiduciary capacity (as is required to create grantor trust status for the trust).[98]

However, Rev. Rul. 2008-22[99] held that such a power of substitution would not be a Section 2036 nor a Section 2038 power as long as the trust instrument or local law required that the trustee has a fiduciary duty to ensure that the properties are, in fact, of equivalent value, and the substitution power cannot be exercised to shift beneficial interests. The ruling did not, however, refer to Section 2042; it isn't clear if this omission was inadvertent or was intentional—on the theory that Section 2042 doesn't contain a "full and adequate consideration" exception that applies to Sections 2036 and 2038. Because of this omission, most practitioners did not include a provision allowing the grantor or insured to hold this power over insurance (including joint, second-to-die insurance) on the grantor's life.[100]

The issuance of Rev. Rul. 2011-28,[101] extending the holding of Rev. Rul. 2008-22 to Section 2042 should put that issue to rest as long as the power is similarly limited.[102] The grantor's ability to retain this power allows greater flexibility in dealing with insurance on the grantor's life by allowing purchases of or substitutions for trust policies on his or her life.

Note that it is possible to give the power of substitution to someone other than the grantor (presumably a non-adverse party) to avoid any Section 2042(2) risk for the grantor but raising the possibility the power would be used by the powerholder to remove the policy from the trust, contrary to the wishes of both the grantor and the beneficiaries. Conceptually, it's difficult to understand how a third party could *re*acquire the policy (because he or she never owned it), but see Ltr. Ruls. 9026036, 9037011, and 9247024, approving such a power as conferring grantor trust status on the trust. However, the same issue would seem to be raised when the grantor contributed cash to the trust that acquired the policy as the initial owner; there, the grantor isn't *re*acquiring the policy because he or she never owned it.

An alternative grantor trust power to consider in an insurance trust would be the power retained by the grantor to borrow from the trust (with adequate interest) but without security, which is a grantor trust power,[103] as long as the trustee doesn't have a general power to lend without security (either under the trust itself or under local law). Finally, the power to add trust beneficiaries (perhaps limited to adding charities) if held by an independent trustee or a trust protector could be considered.[104]

One last issue with the Section 677(a)(3) power is that it can't be given up by the grantor (because it is not a retained power, it is a power granted to the trustee), and it can't safely be given up by the trustee because it would violate the trustee's fiduciary duties to the trust beneficiaries.[105] Both the powers to substitute assets (including, now, policies on the grantor's life) and to borrow without security are retained powers that can be given up by the grantor or taken away by a non-fiduciary (e.g., a trust protector), when it would make sense to terminate grantor trust status for the grantor (perhaps because the cost of paying the tax on trust income becomes burdensome).

For this reason, as already noted, many intentional grantor trusts negate the possible application of the Section 677(a)(3) power by making the use of the trust income to pay premiums discretionary rather than mandatory *and* by requiring an adverse party's consent to any such use.[106] In this way, when the retained grantor trust powers are given up or terminated, it will be clear that the Section 677(a)(3) power won't inadvertently continue to cause the grantor to be taxed on any part of the trust income.[107]

2. *Federal Income Taxation of the Trust and the Grantor During the Grantor's Lifetime*

As discussed earlier, how the trust will be taxed for income tax purposes during the grantor's lifetime is depends on whether the trust or a portion of a trust is treated as a grantor trust or a non-grantor trust. If the trust is treated as a grantor trust, all items of income, deductions, and credits against tax attributable to the trust flow out to the grantor. If the trust is a non-grantor trust, the trust is taxable on the income that is not distributed to the beneficiaries in accordance with the complex trust rules discussed earlier.

There are several advantages to intentionally including certain powers in the trust to make it a grantor trust for income tax purposes. First, the grantor would be able to retain any income tax deduction that would otherwise be available for any interest payments made by the trust with respect to money borrowed against the policy.[108]

Second because a grantor and her or his grantor trust are treated as the same taxpayer for income tax purposes, transactions between them are ignored for income tax purposes.[109] This result allows the trust to buy an appreciating asset from the grantor on an installment basis without recognition of gain by the grantor or taxation of interest on the note[110] and also allows the trust to purchase a policy on the life of the grantor from the grantor without gain or application of the transfer for value rule.[111] On the other hand, as discussed later, if, on termination of the trust's grantor trust status, the trust has outstanding obligations (to the grantor or otherwise), termination of this status would be treated as a sale of the policy for the debt, potentially triggering gain for the grantor.

Finally, a grantor's payment of an income tax liability generated by income from assets in the trust, which is actually his or her liability under the grantor trust rules, should not be treated as a gift to the trust, which would effectively allow the trust to invest on an after-tax basis and would have the economic effect of allowing a grantor to "add" more assets to the trust for the benefit of the trust's beneficiaries.

Although it seems sensible that the grantor's payment of his or her own income tax liability should not be a gift, the Service, in Ltr. Rul. 9444033, stated that, by paying a trust's tax liability, a grantor would be treated as having made an additional transfer to the trust unless the trust instrument provides for the reimbursement of the grantor from trust funds. This position had been subject to considerable criticism, and in Ltr. Rul. 9543049, the Service deleted the language in Ltr. Rul. 9444033 relating to the gift tax implications of the grantor's payment of an income tax liability.

This continued to be, to some extent, an "open issue"; however, until the issuance of Rev. Rul. 2004-64,[112] which put this issue to rest, by holding that no gift resulted from the grantor's payment of the income taxes on income includible in his or her gross income that was generated by his or her grantor trust.

In Rev. Rul. 2004-64, the IRS ruled that when the grantor or a grantor trust pays the income tax attributable to the inclusion of the trust's income in the grantor's taxable income, the grantor is not treated as making a gift of the amount of the tax to the trust beneficiaries because the grantor, not the trust, is liable for the income taxes. The IRS also ruled that if the trust instrument directs the independent trustee to reimburse the grantor for the amount of income tax, the reimbursement is not a gift from the beneficiaries of the trust to the grantor because the reimbursement is mandated by the terms of the trust. However, the grantor's right to be reimbursed from trust assets for the tax is a right to have trust property expended in discharge of the grantor's legal obligation, so the full value of the trust is includible in the grantor's gross estate under Section 2036. This is also true if governing state law requires the trust to reimburse the grantor for the taxes paid unless the trust instrument provides to the contrary.

The ruling further held that a mere authorization in the trust instrument to reimburse the grantor for taxes the grantor pays on income tax attributable to the trust will not cause the trust to be includible in the grantor's estate. However, this assumes "there is no understanding, express or implied, between" the grantor and the trustee regarding the trustee's exercise of discretion. Other facts the ruling notes that might cause estate tax inclusion are a power retained by the grantor to remove the trustee and appoint the grantor and applicable law subjecting the trust assets to the claims of the grantor's creditors.

The safest approach to avoid these issues is to draft the trust instrument to prohibit reimbursement of the grantor. However, compelling reasons to authorize reimbursement may be present in some cases. If so, careful consideration should be given to whether the factors that might cause inclusion in the grantor's gross estate are present. Among other things, the trust instrument must not give the grantor the power to appoint her- or himself as trustee, and the trust should not be created pursuant to the laws of a state that might subject the trust assets to the claims of the grantor's creditors because of the reimbursement provision.

If a potential grantor of a grantor trust wanted to avoid this issue (or if he or she simply did not want to pay "out of pocket" for the income taxes generated by trust income), he or she could include a reimbursement clause in the trust. If a reimbursement clause is included in the trust, however, then if the grantor paid the income tax and was not reimbursed, a gift would result not from payment of the income tax liability but from failure by the grantor to enforce his or her right of reimbursement.

The other, perhaps more certain way, to prevent the grantor of a grantor trust from being taxed on the trust's income, when it becomes an economic issue, is to give the grantor the power to release the power(s) that made the trust a grantor trust (or to give the trustee the power to revoke these powers). Note, however, that if the trust is a grantor trust as to ordinary income because of the Section 677(a)(3) power to pay premiums out of trust income, this power can't be released by the grantor because it isn't a retained power and would not normally be allowed to be revoked by the trustee because it would cause the trust to become taxable. However, a non-fiduciary trust protector could be given the power to amend the trust agreement and, exercising this power, delete the provision that permits the payment of premiums from the income of the trust.

Also note the IRS pronouncement that a grantor trust that contained a "toggling" power, allowing the trustee to turn off grantor trust status and turn it back on, which was used to achieve a tax savings for the grantor, was declared to be a "transaction of interest" in Notice 2007-73[113] and as such was a reportable transaction and subject to taxpayer reporting requirements.[114]

3. *Federal Income Taxation of the Trust and the Trust Beneficiaries After the Grantor's Death*

After the grantor's death, the assets in the trust (the proceeds from the life insurance policy and any other trust property) will either remain in trust or be distributed outright to the beneficiaries.[115] If the assets are distributed to the beneficiaries, the trust will terminate. However, if the proceeds from the insurance policy remain in the trust, the trust and its beneficiaries will be taxed in accordance with the non-grantor trust rules, discussed earlier.

4. *Federal Income Tax Consequences on Termination of the Trust's Status as a Grantor Trust (Either at the Grantor's Death or During His or Her Lifetime)*

a. The Trust's Outstanding Liabilities

Assuming the trust is drafted as a grantor trust, it will cease to be a grantor trust upon the death of the grantor[116] or upon termination of the power(s) that caused it to be treated as a grantor trust during the grantor's life.[117] As a result, thereafter, the trust will no longer be disregarded for income tax purposes and instead will be treated as a separate taxable entity.

As discussed later, on termination of the trust's grantor status during the grantor's lifetime, if the trust then has any outstanding liabilities (to the grantor or to a third party[118]), the termination of that status will be treated as a sale of the policy by the grantor to the trust in exchange for the liability. This deemed sale would generate gain to the extent the outstanding liability exceeded the grantor's basis in the policy (as discussed later). For this reason, as noted earlier, consideration should be given to creating the trust as a non-grantor trust but, of course, that would mean the interest paid to or accrued for the grantor would be taxable to the grantor—an undesirable result.[119]

There is less certainty about the income tax consequences of termination of grantor trust status as a result of the death of the grantor when the trust has outstanding liabilities (to the grantor or to a third party[120]). As discussed later, some commentators believe that the grantor's death and resultant termination of grantor trust status have no income tax consequences; under this analysis, death is not an event that triggers gain recognition. Another possible result, and the one that the IRS would likely adopt, is that the income tax consequences on the death of the grantor are the same as those that are deemed to occur when grantor trust status is terminated during the grantor's life, as set forth in the Regulations under Section 1001 and other authorities.[121] Under this analysis, the income tax consequences would be the same, whether termination of grantor trust status is a result of the grantor's death or a termination of the applicable grantor trust power(s) during the grantor's life when the trust had any outstanding liabilities.

In either event, as discussed later, it seems that, under the grantor trust rules, the donor and the ILIT would have the same starting basis in the policy—the premiums loaned—so there would be little or no taxable gain resulting from termination of grantor trust status in any case.

b. Termination of the Trust's Grantor Trust Status During the Life of the Grantor

On termination of the trust's grantor trust status during the grantor's life, the grantor will be deemed to have transferred to the trust for income tax (but not for gift or GST tax) purposes the assets of the trust in this case, the policy, in exchange for the liabilities of the trust.[122]

Under the Section 1001 Regulations, there are immediate income tax consequences to the grantor when grantor trust status is terminated if the trust has any outstanding liabilities (again, whether to the grantor or to a third party[123]), and these liabilities exceed the grantor's basis in the assets deemed transferred to the trust; however, as in any other capital asset sale context, the grantor recognizes gain *only* to the extent the liabilities of the trust exceed the grantor's basis in the assets deemed transferred to the trust. Under the general rule of Treas. Reg. Sec. 1.1001-2(a)(1), the amount realized from a sale or other disposition of property includes the amount of liabilities from which the transferor is discharged as a result of such sale or disposition; in this case, the trust's deemed assumption of the grantor's liabilities is treated as a discharge of the grantor's liabilities in consideration for the assets (in this case, the policy) that the grantor is deemed to have transferred to the trust.

However, Treas. Reg. Sec. 1.1001-2(a)(3) provides an exception to this rule when a liability is incurred for purposes of acquiring property and is not taken into account in determining the transferor's basis in such property (e.g., based on a literal interpretation of then regulation provision when the loan is between the grantor and his or her grantor trust and thus is ignored for income tax purposes under Rev. Rul. 85-13[124]). Under these circumstances, the assumed liability will not be included in the amount realized by the transferor on termination of the trust's grantor status and therefore should not cause recognition of gain.[125]

Example 5 of Treas. Reg. Sec. 1.1001-2(c), noted earlier, illustrates what is deemed to occur on termination of grantor trust status during the grantor's life. In the example, a grantor was considered to be the partner of a partnership in which the grantor trust held an interest. Upon termination of grantor trust status on the renunciation of a grantor trust power, a constructive transfer of the partnership interest to the trust was deemed to occur. The example concludes that the grantor is required to recognize gain to the extent the allocable share of partnership liabilities assumed by the trust exceeds the grantor's basis in the partnership interest. Similarly, in *Madorin v. Commissioner*,[126] a grantor transferred to a grantor trust an interest in a partnership that held encumbered assets. The grantor deducted the net losses generated by the partnership until the trustee eliminated the power that had caused the trust to be a grantor trust. The court held that the grantor was thereupon released from his share of the underlying partnership liabilities and recognized gain to the extent that those liabilities exceeded his basis in the partnership interest.

In applying the general rule of Example 5 of Treas. Reg. Sec. 1.1001-2(a)(1) to a premium financing transaction with the grantor, on the termination of the status of the trust as a grantor trust, the grantor will be deemed to have transferred the life insurance policy to the trust in exchange for the trust's assumption of the grantor's loan to the trust in connection with the trust's acquisition of the policy. Note the issues discussed later, as to exactly when the deemed sale takes place, whether liabilities to the grantor trigger the deemed sale rule, and whether termination of grantor trust status at the grantor's death is subject to the deemed sale rule. Under the general rule, the grantor will realize income to the extent the liability (i.e., the amount of the grantor's outstanding loan on termination of the trust's grantor trust status) assumed by the trust exceeds the grantor's basis in the policy.[127]

If the exception of Treas. Reg. Sec. 1.1001-2(a)(3) applies, because the liability (the loan) was incurred by the trust in connection with the acquisition of the policy and is not taken into account in determining the grantor's basis in the policy—which would be true of a loan between a grantor and his or her grantor trust—then no income will be realized by the grantor on termination of the trust's grantor trust status even if the liability deemed assumed by the trust exceeds the grantor's basis in the policy (however measured).[128]

However, even if the exception contained in Treas. Reg. Sec. 1.1001-2(a)(3) does not apply in the insurance trust situation, the termination of the trust's grantor trust status still would not result in a recognition of gain by the grantor if the liability incurred by the trust to acquire the policy does not exceed the grantor's basis in the policy. Because the trust is treated as a grantor trust and therefore considered a disregarded entity for income tax purposes,[129] the grantor's basis in the policy should be the same as the trust's basis in the policy. Whether the trust's (and therefore the grantor's) basis in the policy is the premiums it paid, less any non-taxable distributions (e.g., policy dividends in traditional whole life policies or withdrawals up to basis in universal life policies) or whether that basis is further reduced by the cost of the insurance protection provided to the trust (however measured) depends on whether the holding of Rev. Rul. 2009-13[130] applies outside of the life settlement sale context.

One issue that may arise upon the termination of the grantor trust status of an insurance trust during the grantor or insured's lifetime that borrowed from the grantor to finance the premiums and the resultant deemed transfer of the policy in exchange for the release of the grantor's liability is whether a transfer for value[131] of the policy under Section 101(a)(2) has occurred when the grantor trust becomes a non-grantor trust.

Under the transfer for value rule of Section 101(a)(2), life insurance proceeds in excess of the transferee's investment in the contract will be taxed as ordinary income if there has been a transfer of the policy or any interest in the policy for valuable consideration during the insured's lifetime. If a policy is transferred for value during the insured's lifetime, the amount includable in taxable income is the death benefit minus (1) the actual value of any consideration received (in this case, relief from the liability) and (2) premiums and other amounts subsequently paid by transferee (which in this case would not occur).

Transfers for value include the sale of a policy, a transfer of rights to the policy proceeds for consideration, and transfers of policies subject to loans.[132] Transfers are broadly defined for this purpose, but there isn't any authority holding that transfers for this purpose are broadly enough defined to include a *deemed* transfer for income tax purposes that does not involve a physical transfer of the policy or an interest in a policy—this deemed "transfer" does not change who will benefit from the policy proceeds, which is the concern that underlies the transfer for value concept. See Ltr. Rul. 9410034, which held that when a partnership was terminated for tax purposes because 50% of the partners (who would have benefited from the proceeds) changed, there was a transfer for value of its policies; here, however, there is no change in the trust beneficiaries as a result of termination of the trust's grantor trust status during the grantor's life.

c. Termination of the Trust's Grantor Trust Status at the Death of the Grantor

This issue is especially critical for premium financing transactions because unlike other transactions between grantors and their grantor trusts—installment sales, for instance—it is likely the premium financing loan will be outstanding at the grantor's death, and there is much less incentive than in installment sales to have intentionally terminated grantor trust status of the trust by terminating the retained powers, which made the trust a grantor trust during the grantor's life to avoid the grantor having to continue to pay tax on trust income.

As discussed earlier, there is substantial uncertainty and debate among commentators regarding the income tax consequences on termination of grantor trust status as a result of the grantor's death when the trust has outstanding liabilities at that time.[133] Some commentators view the transfer of assets that is deemed to occur on the grantor's death as tantamount to a testamentary transfer of the assets to the trust.[134] Under this theory, a gain-on-death rule is contrary to the rule of Section 1001, and accordingly, no gain should be triggered on the deemed transfer of the assets to the trust in exchange for the trust's assumption of the liability upon the death of the grantor.[135]

On the other hand, other commentators believe that when grantor trust status is terminated by the grantor's death, the deemed transfer of the assets to the trust triggers gain to the extent any assumed liability exceeds the grantor's basis in the assets transferred, just as in the case of termination of grantor trust status during the grantor's life.[136] It is argued that this will be the IRS position as well. But see CCA 200923024, commenting on the example in the Section 1001 Regulations stating that the authorities are ". . . narrow, in so far as [they] only [affect] intervivos lapses of grantor trust status, not that caused by the death of the grantor, which is generally not treated as an income tax event."

Thus, under this analysis, as discussed earlier, on the grantor's death and the corresponding termination of grantor trust status of the trust, the grantor will be deemed to have transferred the life insurance policy to the trust in exchange for the assumption by the trust of the loan incurred in connection with the acquisition of the policy. Under the general rule of Treas. Reg. Sec. 1.1001-2(a)(1), the grantor will recognize gain to the extent the liability assumed by the trust exceeds the grantor's basis in the policy (as discussed earlier). However, if it is determined that the exception of Treas. Reg. Sec. 1.1001-2(a)(3) applies, because the liability was incurred in connection with the acquisition of the life insurance policy and was not taken into account in determining the transferor's basis, then no gain will be recognized by the grantor (or her or his estate) on termination of the trust's grantor trust status even if the liability deemed assumed exceeds the grantor's basis in the policy.[137]

The open issue here is *precisely* when the deemed transfer takes place—at the moment of, the moment before, or the moment after the event ending grantor trust status, in this case, the grantor or insured's death? There isn't any direct authority on this issue in the context of a US domestic trust, other than the provision in the Section 1001 regulations, discussed earlier, which indicates the deemed sale takes place "when" (at the moment when?) grantor trust status ends; there is, however, an arguably analogous area—the termination of grantor trust status of a foreign trust taxed as a grantor trust, under Section 679. There, Treas. Reg. Sec. 1.684-2(e) provides that when any portion of a foreign trust ceases to be treated as owned by a grantor for income tax purposes (including, as Example (2) of that regulation section provides, the death of the grantor), the grantor is treated as having transferred the property to the trust, recognizing gain on any appreciation in the property, *immediately before (but on the same day as)* the trust stops being owned by the grantor for income tax purposes.[138]

If the rule of the Section 684 regulations applied more generally, that is, outside the foreign trust area to a US domestic insurance trust, it would seem to solve the issue because when the policy was deemed transferred to the trust—the moment *before* the grantor's death—the trust would still be a grantor trust, and therefore, there would be no gain to recognize under the theory of Rev. Rul. 85-13.[139] In the transfer for value context, if the rule were that the policy was deemed to have been transferred immediately before the grantor's death, the trust would still be a grantor trust, its basis would be the grantor's basis, and the transfer would be deemed to be to the insured—in either case, qualifying for an exemption to the transfer for value rule.[140]

5. *The Federal Income Taxation of Accrued Interest*

a. The Original Issue Discount Rules

When adequate interest (based on the AFR) is not paid on a debt instrument or when a debt instrument does not require the current payment of interest, interest income is imputed to the holder of the debt or the seller of the property under the OID rules of Sections 1272, 1273, and 1274.[141] Briefly, Section 1273 provides that the amount of OID is equal to the difference between the issue price of an instrument and its stated redemption price at maturity.[142] For deferred payment sales, the OID rules apply if (1) the stated redemption price at maturity for the debt instrument exceeds the stated principal amount (where there is adequate stated interest) or the imputed principal amount (in any other case)[143] and (2) some or all the payments under the instrument are due more than 6 months after the date of the sale.

In general, holders of debt instruments must include in income the sum of the daily portion of OID determined for each day during the tax year the instrument is held,[144] and the OID rules place the holder of a debt instrument on the accrual method of accounting as to any interest (whether stated or imputed) not paid currently. Concomitantly, Section 163(e) generally allows an interest deduction (to the extent not otherwise disallowed by some other Code provision) to the issuer of a debt instrument for the daily portions of OID during the taxable year.

Similarly, Section 7872 provides rules applicable to below-market loans and provides for the imputation of interest in the case of certain loans[145] when stated interest (in the case of a demand loan) or the yield (in the case of a term loan) is less than the AFR. Under Section 7872, loans that bear below-market rate interest or no interest are generally recharacterized as arm's-length transactions in which the lender is treated as having made a loan to the borrower bearing the AFR. There is then deemed to be a transfer in the form of gift, dividend, contribution to capital, compensation, or other form of payment (depending on the nature of the loan) from the lender to the borrower, which in turn is retransferred by the borrower to the lender to satisfy the accruing interest.[146] In the case of a term loan (other than a gift term loan), there is an imputed transfer from the lender to the borrower in an amount equal to the excess of the amount lent over the present value of all payments required under the loan (discounted at the applicable AFR).[147] Such loan is treated as having OID equal to the amount of the imputed transfer (i.e., deemed OID).[148] In the case of a demand loan or a gift loan, the imputed interest amount is the "foregone interest," as defined in Section 7872(e)(2).

b. Income Tax Treatment of Accrued OID During the Grantor's Life

Assuming the trust is a grantor trust and the trust borrows funds from the grantor, any OID (or deemed OID on a below-market loan) accrued on the loan during the grantor's life will be disregarded for income tax purposes. The OID rules, which would ordinarily apply in this situation to impute interest to the grantor on a current basis, do not apply under the rationale of Rev. Rul. 85-13[149] because the trust is a grantor trust.[150]

In Rev. Rul. 85-13, the IRS held that a grantor trust is disregarded as an entity for income tax purposes, and the grantor is deemed to own the assets of the trust for income tax purposes. In the ruling, the grantor trust sold appreciated stock to the grantor in exchange for an installment note. The IRS stated that because the grantor is considered the owner of the grantor trust under the grantor trust provisions and thus is both the maker and the owner of the installment note, the purported purchase by the grantor of the appreciated stock is not recognized as a purchase for income tax purposes.[151] Similarly, in Ltr. Rul. 9535026, the grantor transferred stock to a grantor trust in exchange for a promissory note paying a market rate of interest for 20 years followed by a balloon payment of principal. The IRS, relying on Rev. Rul. 85-13, determined that in addition to no gain or loss recognition, the grantor trust could not deduct the interest payments, and the grantor did not have interest income attributable to the promissory note.

See also Ltr. Rul. 9519029, citing Rev. Rul. 85-13, which concluded that no gain or loss will be recognized to the grantor or the grantor trust on the transfer of assets by the grantor to the trust to fund the trust, on the transfer of any property from the trust to the grantor in payment of any annuity installments, or on the substitution by the grantor of assets of the grantor for assets of the trust.[152]

Accordingly, under Rev. Rul. 85-13 and subsequent rulings, transactions between a grantor and a grantor trust are ignored for income tax purposes. Consequently, if the trust owes money to the grantor, there is no debt for income tax purposes because the debt runs both to and from the grantor and cannot represent a true indebtedness. Thus, the grantor will not recognize interest income, and the grantor trust will not be allowed an interest deduction for interest paid on the "disregarded" loan. Moreover because any debt instruments between the grantor and the grantor trust are disregarded for income tax purposes, no OID (or deemed OID) can arise during the grantor's life. Accordingly, no OID (or deemed OID) is accrued nor taxed during the grantor's life on debts between the grantor and the grantor trust; for the year of the grantor's death, the OID accrued that year would be taxed on the grantor's final income tax return (because the trust wasn't a grantor trust that year).

c. Accrued OID as Income in Respect of a Decedent

Although there appears to be some uncertainty and debate regarding the income tax consequences of OID (or deemed OID) on termination of the trust's grantor trust status as a result of the grantor's death,[153] it appears that pre-death accrued OID (or deemed OID) on a loan (or deferred payment sale) from a grantor to a grantor trust should not constitute income in respect of a decedent (IRD) in the hands of the grantor's estate or heirs. Treas. Reg. Sec. 1.691(a)-1(b) provides that, in general, IRD "refers to those amounts to which a decedent was entitled as gross income but which were not properly includible in computing his taxable income for the taxable year ending with the date of his death or for a previous taxable year under the method of accounting employed by the decedent." Thus, the term IRD is understood to include items of income that, at the time of death, the decedent had earned or accrued but not yet received for income tax purposes.

As discussed earlier, the OID rules do not operate during the grantor's life on debts between the grantor and the grantor trust for income tax purposes because the trust and thus the debt are disregarded for income tax purposes. Consequently, OID on the disregarded debt is not taxed to the grantor, nor deducted by the grantor trust, during the grantor's life. Because pre-death OID did not constitute income to the grantor while living, these amounts (the accrued OID) should not constitute IRD in the hands of the grantor's estate or successors.[154] To do otherwise would tax something after death, the accrued OID, that would never have been taxed had the grantor continued to live.

6. Planning the Grantor Trust Status of the Trust

Given both the potential advantages and risks associated with the trust's grantor trust status, as described earlier, careful consideration should be given to this status when planning and drafting the trust.

Although it's difficult to generalize, when the insured is the lender, it's likely the trust would be created as a grantor trust from the insured's point of view to prevent the insured from recognizing the receipt of interest from the trust as income or the recognition of OID as income each year, when interest on the loan is accrued and will be paid at the insured's death. In addition, when grantor trust status is important for another planning reason, such as use of the trust as the buyer in an installment sale of appreciating assets from the grantor, which is disregarded for income tax purposes under Rev. Rul. 85-13,[155] or as the buyer of a life insurance policy from the insured-grantor, in an attempt to avoid both the 3-year "look-back" rule of Section 2035 and the transfer for value rule of Section 101(a)(2), the planning will likely require grantor trust status for the trust despite these risks.

On the other hand, when the lender is a third party and the trust is not likely to own any assets other than the policy during the insured's lifetime, creating the trust as a non-grantor trust would eliminate all risks relating to the termination of the trust's grantor status at the insured's death if the liability to the third party is then outstanding and would have no disadvantages.

More difficult choices are raised in situations when the insured is the lender, but it seems unlikely that the trust's obligation to the insured will be repaid before his or her death and in trusts involved in premium financing arrangements with third-party lenders, when the trust is going to be funded with substantial income producing assets during the insured's lifetime. In either of those cases, the risks associated with grantor trust status if the loan is outstanding at the insured's death will need to be weighed against the current income tax cost of requiring the insured to report the interest received (or accrued) as income (where he or she is the lender) or losing the opportunity to have the insured pay the income tax on trust-generated income with no gift tax consequences (when the lender is a third party).

Again, the safest way to assure non-grantor trust status for an insurance trust by avoiding the application of Section 677(a)(3) is to require the approval of an adverse party to the discretionary trustee power to use trust income to pay premiums on a policy on the grantor's (or his or her spouse's) life and then obtain such approval in advance of using trust income to pay premiums on such a policy.

G. Treatment of the Loan from the Grantor to the Trust as Bona Fide Debt for Federal Tax Purposes

Finally, there is the issue of whether a private premium financing note will be respected as bona fide debt for federal income and gift tax purposes. As discussed later, a typical private premium financing obligation should be treated as debt for federal tax purposes, both under the Final Split-Dollar Regulations and under general tax principles.

1. The Final Split-Dollar Regulations

Under the Final Split-Dollar Regulations, a payment made pursuant to a split-dollar life insurance arrangement is treated as a loan for federal tax purposes, and the owner and non-owner are treated, respectively, as the borrower and the lender if, among other requirements, the payment is a loan under general principles of federal tax law or if it is not a loan under general principles of federal tax law (e.g., because of the non-recourse nature of the obligation or otherwise), a reasonable person nevertheless would expect the payment to be repaid in full to the non-owner (whether with or without interest).[156] In a typical private premium financing transaction, a reasonable person would expect the premium payment to be repaid in full, including interest, by the trust. Such a loan, since because the parties in a premium financing arrangement expect repayment of the amounts loaned, if respected under the Final Split-Dollar Regulations, will also be respected for gift tax purposes because the preamble to the Regulations states that Regulations apply for gift tax purposes, including private split-dollar life insurance arrangements.

In addition, even if the repayment obligation were to be characterized as something other than debt under the more general principles of federal tax law (e.g., characterized as proceeds from the sale of the policy or a fee payment for the use of the insured's life), an argument could be made, based on the plain language of the Regulations, that the payment is nevertheless treated as a loan for all federal tax purposes. The preamble to the Regulations, in response to commentators questioning whether the provision was necessary, states:

> [t]he IRS and Treasury recognize that, in the earlier years during which a split-dollar life insurance arrangement is in effect, policy surrender and load charges may significantly reduce the policy's cash surrender value, resulting in under-collateralization of a non-owner's right to be repaid its premium payments.

> Therefore, so long as a reasonable person would expect the payment to be repaid in full, the payment is a split-dollar loan under §1.7872-15, rather than a transfer under §1.61-22(b)(5) on the date the payment is made.

Despite the treatment as a loan for federal tax purposes under the Regulations, however, it is unclear whether this Regulation will govern in a circumstance when a payment could be properly characterized as something other than debt (e.g., equity, proceeds from a sale, a fee payment) outside of the split-dollar context. On one hand, the Service should not be able to treat a split-dollar loan as something other than debt for other tax purposes if the Regulations required the taxpayers to treat the payment as a payment with respect to a loan for purposes of computing interest income and interest expense. However, given the "elective" nature of the Regulations (based generally on ownership of the policy), it seems an argument could be made that taxpayers should not be able to circumvent other unfavorable tax consequences by merely electing to apply the Regulations.

2. *General Principles of Federal Tax Law*

Hundreds of cases have analyzed whether a purported debt obligation is bona fide for federal income tax purposes. These cases involve a variety of circumstances, including the deductibility of interest payments with respect to a purported debt obligation, the characterization of an obligation as debt versus equity, the proper amount of "debt" included in a taxpayer's adjusted basis, and whether an amount related to a purported debt obligation received by the taxpayer is included in income or if paid by the taxpayer is deductible as an expense. Premium financing by the grantor or insured should satisfy the general principles established in these income tax cases, as discussed later.

Courts have held "[w]hether a transfer of money creates a bona fide debt depends upon the existence of an intent by both parties, substantially contemporaneous to the time of such transfer, to establish an enforceable obligation of repayment."[157] In *Professional Services v. CIR*, the taxpayer argued that the payment did constitute a real economic cost because he borrowed the purchase price and the note constituted bona fide indebtedness. The Court disagreed and stated:

> We hold that petitioners have failed to meet their burden of proof on this point. In fact, the substantial weight of the evidence leads directly to the conclusion that no true liability ever existed. The terms and circumstances of the "loan" itself, clearly demonstrate that the "loan" was not bona fide. Mr. Bumpus testified to the

> effect that, from the outset, it was intended that petitioner would not be required to pay any amounts to the lending entity on the note. Rather, it was intended that the "promissory note" would be placed within the "borrower's" control prior to any payments falling due on the "note."[158]

To be valid for federal income tax purposes, a debt obligation must be a legally enforceable obligation to pay money.[159] State law is controlling on the issue whether a debt obligation is legally enforceable.[160] In general, under state law, a debt obligation is legally enforceable only if it is given in exchange for consideration (i.e., money or other valuable rights or property).

Another important factor analyzed by the Tax Court to determine whether a debt obligation is bona fide is the likelihood the debt will be satisfied. For example, in *Waddell v. Commissioner*,[161] the court pointed out that support for the position that a non-recourse debt is included in a taxpayer's adjusted basis is predicated on the assumption that the debt will be repaid in full. The court identified and analyzed two primary approaches used by courts regarding this assumption. The first major approach looks at the fair market value of the property in relation to the stated purchase price and/or the principal amount of the indebtedness. This line of cases treats a non-recourse obligation as a true debt only if the acquired property reasonably secures payment of the obligation; when the non-recourse obligation is not adequately secured, a purchaser would acquire no equity in the property and therefore would have no economic incentive to repay the note.

The second major approach holds that an obligation, even if recourse, will not be treated as a true debt where payment, according to its terms, is too contingent.[162] The court in *Waddell* noted that this "contingent obligation" approach was applied in recent tax shelter cases involving non-recourse loans when the principal was payable out of the exploitation of the asset purchased with the loan.[163]

The court in *Waddell* also noted that these approaches are complementary and represent efforts by the courts to validate from objective criteria the assumption upon which a valid non-recourse debt (for tax purposes) is predicated—the assumption that the obligation will be paid. The court concluded "[a] nonrecourse debt will be recognized for tax purposes only if it appears likely from all the facts and circumstances that the obligation will be paid."[164]

The court in *Waddell* determined the taxpayer's purchase money note must be tested under these principles. The court noted the value of the property at the inception of the transaction and throughout the term is of great importance in evaluating the likelihood of payment. The court concluded the appropriate approach is

> to look at the transaction based on the facts and circumstances at its inception—including reasonable revenue projections based on objective criteria and the value of the security at the time the lender has a right to proceed against the security for payment—and determine whether it is likely that the note will be paid. If we cannot conclude at the outset of the transaction that payment of the note is likely, then the note is too contingent to be recognized for tax purposes.[165]

Under traditional debt–equity analysis, characterization of a "loan" as debt or equity is based on the facts and circumstances of the transaction.[166] In this context, the courts and the Service define "debt" as an unqualified obligation to pay a sum certain at a reasonably close maturity date along with a fixed percentage of interest payable regardless of the debtor's income or lack thereof.[167] The essential inquiry in characterizing a contribution as debt or equity is whether the contributor intended the sum to be subject to the risks of the business or to be repayable regardless of the venture's profitability.[168] (Characterization depends on the taxpayer's true intent as evidenced by the particular circumstances.)

The issue of the intent of the parties in a private loan setting has been most frequently litigated in the Tax Court, which has generally recognized valid, enforceable intra-family notes as loans for federal tax purposes, particularly when they were secured.[169] As the Tax Court in *Hunt v. CIR*[170] stated:

> In the context of intra-family loans, however, our focus is much more on the intent of the parties. Unlike the debt-equity cases where the corporation and the shareholders share the same interest in creating debt for tax purposes, in these instances, even though the parties are related, the "lender" and the "borrower" have conflicting interests. In these cases, the children benefit but the parents suffer if the transfers are characterized as gifts. Conversely, if the transfers are characterized as loans, the parents are advantaged but the children risk having substantial income from the relief of indebtedness.

However, an intra-family loan may not be respected for federal tax purposes if loan payments are forgiven on a regular basis or the terms of the loan are not enforced; in these situations, the Service may argue that the loan must be disregarded *ab initio*, so the loaned amounts are treated as gifts when made. That result follows, according to the Service, if the "lender" intended from the outset to forgive the notes that he or she received.[171] For example, in *Deal v. Comm'r*,[172] the Court found that the notes executed by the transferee daughters "were not intended to be enforced and were not intended as consideration for the transfer by the petitioner, and that, in substance, the transfer of the property was by gift."[173]

Finally, as discussed earlier, the provisions of the Final Split-Dollar Regulations that treat a split-dollar loan as a loan for all federal tax purposes even if it would not be treated as a loan under general principles of federal tax law as long as a reasonable person would expect the loan to be repaid, assuming there is compliance with the representation requirement of these Regulations, should apply to these loans.

H. The Grantor's Guarantee of Third-Party Loans to the Trust or a Pledge of Collateral as Security for Such Loans to the Trust

Under Section 2042(2), the proceeds of a life insurance policy insuring the life of the decedent are included in the decedent's estate if the decedent possessed any "incidents of ownership" in the policy on his or her death. The term "incidents of ownership" is broadly defined to include all rights to the economic benefits of the policy, such as the right to name or change beneficiaries, the right to surrender the policy, the right to pledge the policy for a loan, or the right to obtain a loan from the insurer against the cash surrender value of the policy.

Section 2035(a) provides, in part, that if a decedent makes a transfer of property within 3 years of his or her death (for less than full consideration) and if before the transfer, the property would have been included in his or her estate under Section 2042, the property will be included in his or her estate under Section 2035. Thus, if a decedent transfers a policy (or any incidents of ownership in a policy) within 3 years before his or her death (for less than full consideration), the policy proceeds will be included in his or her estate for estate tax purposes.

Accordingly, the first issue raised by the donor or insured's guarantee of the trust's third-party loan is whether the insured, as a result of guaranteeing the loan, would be deemed to hold any incident of ownership in the policy. As long as the guarantee, either explicitly or under applicable state law, does not give the grantor any rights to the policy (in the form of subrogation rights and so on), the grantor should not be deemed to hold any incidents of ownership in the policy as a result of the guarantee,[174] so the proceeds of the policy should not be included in his or her estate (assuming, of course, that the trust is properly drafted to prevent the grantor from holding any incidents of ownership).

The insured's guarantee of a loan used to pay premiums on a policy on the insured's life (or pledge of assets as security for such a loan) should not cause inclusion of the policy proceeds in the insured's estate under Section 2042 as long as the guarantee does not directly grant incidents of ownership in the policy to the guarantor, in the form of subrogation or other similar rights. Because a guarantee typically includes rights of subrogation, however, any guarantee agreement must specifically limit these subrogation rights, as they apply to the policy, so that the insured's rights in the policy as subrogee are limited to the right to receive a portion of the policy cash value, if the policy is surrendered, or to receive a portion of the policy death benefit upon the insured's death.[175]

It has been suggested by some commentators that if the trust pledges the policy as security for the loan, which is guaranteed by the grantor, the grantor receives some benefit from the trust's pledge of the policy—presumably because it is then less likely that he or she will be required to make payments under his or her guarantee—which, they argue, constitutes an incident of ownership in the policy. However, we found no authority for this proposition, and the existing authority seems to suggest otherwise.

As a practical matter, there is no apparent benefit to the settlor as a result of the trust's pledge of the policy it owns as security for its own loan. The fact that the "value" of what the settlor may be providing the trust in terms of his or her guarantee may be reduced does not mean that the settlor affirmatively receives a benefit as a result of the transaction. However, in some cases, particularly when the acquisition of a policy on the insured's life (to be owned by a third party) and a subsequent pledge of the policy by the owner as security for a loan to the insured by an unrelated lender is part of an integrated transaction, courts have held the policy was includible in the insured's estate.[176]

On the other hand, when the transaction is not integrated to the degree it was, for instance, in *Pritchard*,[177] other courts have concluded that when a third-party owner of a policy pledged the policy as security directly for the insured's loan, then because the decision to make the pledge was within the discretion of the third-party owner and not a right held by the insured, the insured had no incident of ownership as a result of the pledge.[178]

The fact that the source of the policy premiums could be argued to be coming indirectly from the decedent should likewise not cause inclusion of the policy proceeds in the decedent's estate under Section 2042. In Ltr. Rul. 9809032, the Service considered a situation in which the decedent had *directly* loaned funds to an irrevocable insurance trust he created, which were used by the trustees to pay the premiums on a policy insuring the decedent's life that was owned by the trust. The executors of the decedent's estate requested a ruling that the decedent did not hold any incidents of ownership in the policy for purposes of Section 2042(2) as a result of having loaned the funds used to pay the premiums on the policy.

The Service noted that under the terms of the trust, the decedent held no incidents of ownership in the policy, nor did he transfer any incidents of ownership in the policy during the 3-year period before his death. Therefore, none of the policy proceeds were included in his estate under Section 2042(2). The Service further noted that the fact that the decedent, through loans, had provided the funds for payment of the policy premiums was irrelevant because "payment of premiums is irrelevant in determining whether a decedent retained any incidents of ownership in the policy proceeds."[179]

For its holding regarding the irrelevancy of payment of premiums in an "incidents of ownership" analysis, the Service in Ltr. Rul. 9809032 cited *Estate of Leder v. Commissioner*[180] and *Estate of Headrick v. Commissioner*.[181] The primary focus of these cases was inclusion of policy proceeds under Section 2035 (which, when dealing with life insurance proceeds, obviously requires an analysis of Section 2042). They are among those cases in which the Tax Court rejected arguments by the Service, largely made under Section 2035 (which generally included in a decedent's estate any transfer made within 3 years of death), that an insured's direct or, in some cases, indirect, payment of premiums should be treated as a "transfer" subject to Section 2035, which, if made within 3 years of the decedent's death, would cause the policy proceeds to be included in the decedent's estate. *Estate of Leder*[182] was the first case to consider this issue based on the then current Section 2035, and the court concluded that as amended, for Section 2035(d)(1)—now Section 2035(a)—to apply to insurance, first Section 2042 had to apply to the insurance.

When the policy had been originally applied for and owned by the insured's spouse, as in *Estate of Leder*,[183] the insured never owned (and transferred) the policy; therefore, Section 2035 did not apply to cause inclusion of the policy proceeds.

As is indirectly supported by its statement in Ltr. Rul. 9809032, the Service seems to agree with this basic analysis—the determining factor in an analysis of whether the proceeds of a policy insuring a decedent's life are includible under Section 2035 is whether the decedent possessed incidents of ownership in the actual policy within the 3-year period before his or her date of death. The fact that he or she may have provided the source of premium payments on a policy on his or her life within that 3-year period is irrelevant. Here, the decedent is even further removed from the premium payments because she or he will merely be guaranteeing a third-party loan used to fund these payments. In Ltr. Rul. 9809032, the Service ruled that a direct loan by the insured to the policy owner in the amount of the premium payments did not cause inclusion of the policy on his life purchased by the borrower in the insured's estate for estate tax purposes; accordingly, having the insured guarantee similar loans should not cause inclusion of these proceeds in his or her estate for estate purposes under Section 2042.

Most commentators would agree that if an individual is required to actually make payments to a lender pursuant to his or her guarantee (or if pledged assets are used to satisfy the loan),[184] then assuming the guarantee was not made for adequate consideration, the guarantor's payment will be treated as a gift to the borrower, less perhaps any amounts received by the guarantor from the borrower under the guarantor's subrogation rights.[185] Similarly, if the guarantor gratuitously pays either the loan interest or principal, it would also be treated as a gift to the borrower. The issue addressed here is whether there is an *immediate* gift to the borrower when the guarantor merely guarantees the loan (or the pledgor merely pledges assets as security for the loan).

There is very little authority on this issue; in fact, what little authority there was (with which we and most commentators had disagreed) has now been withdrawn; this appears to be an area in which there is an apparent absence of authority. Most of the discussion centers on two Ltr. Ruls.: 9113009 and 9409018.

In Ltr. Rul. 9113009, the Service took the position that a father's guarantee of his child's loan constituted a gift to the child when the guarantee was made. The Service also concluded that if guarantees were outstanding at the father's death, then because the marital trust created under the father's estate plan might be required to make payments on a guarantee, the marital trust would not qualify for the marital deduction.

In Ltr. Rul. 9409018, the Service reconsidered some of the issues raised in Ltr. Rul. 9113009 and ruled that the marital deduction would not be disallowed, although it could still presumably be reduced by the estimated "value" of the contingent liabilities under the guarantees if other assets of the estate available to satisfy the guarantor's potential obligations were valued at less than such amount. The Service withdrew Ltr. Rul. 9113009, *but, importantly, it did not further address the issue of whether the father's guarantee of the loans would constitute a current gift.*

Another possible reason for the absence of any other authority in this area may be due to a similar issue raised in the S corporation arena. In fact, the Service's position in the S corporation area may provide some support for the position that a mere guarantee is not a current gift.

Shareholders of an S corporation who are asked to guarantee loans to the S corporation have long attempted to take the position that their stock or debt basis in the corporation should be increased when they personally guarantee loans to the corporation. Courts, however, have almost unanimously rejected this argument,[186] holding instead that their basis will not be increased until payments are actually made on the loan pursuant to the guarantee.[187]

Commentators have argued that guarantees by S corporation shareholders of the corporation's debts should be recognized as a current "economic outlay" and be given a current value so that the shareholder's basis in the stock or debt of the corporation will be increased. Commentators have offered several methods of valuing the guarantees, although they recognize it is a difficult task.[188]

Shareholders of S corporations who have guaranteed loans of their corporations must have anticipated using Ltr. Rul. 9113009 as support for their position that guarantees should be given value for basis purposes when made. Similarly, in the gift or guarantee area, the Service's long-standing argument that guarantees by S corporation shareholders do not involve a current economic outlay, which can be added to basis (and the courts' acceptance of it) should be able to be used as support for the position that personal guarantees do not involve a current economic outlay or transfer of property by the guarantor for gift tax purposes.

In summary, the law addressing the issue of gift or guarantees is quite sparse, and the Service may have strong reasons for abandoning its once-stated position on the gift tax treatment of guarantees. Nevertheless, it is clear that a guarantee provides a benefit to the borrower even if it is intangible and not subject to simple valuation (somewhat like the intangible—but valuable benefit—of being born into a wealthy family). Therefore, anyone contemplating guaranteeing a loan should be aware of the Service's once-stated (then withdrawn) position that the guarantee itself was a gift for federal gift tax consequences and should know the potential consequences resulting from this position being asserted and sustained.[189]

I. The Application of the Recent Tax Court Cases on Economic Benefit Generational Split-Dollar Cases to Loan Regime Arrangements

1. *See the more detailed discussion of these cases in Section V.J., below.*

2. *The Sections 2036(a)(2) and 2038(a)(1) Issue*

In the *Cahill* case,[190] the Tax Court determined that the generational economic benefit split-dollar transaction involved there[191] was not for adequate and full consideration by comparing the amount of the advances made by the decedent to the fair market value of the receivables, as reported on the estate's federal estate tax return. The result should be different for an intra-family split-dollar loan regime transaction, given the objective, present value methodology for valuing notes in intra-family transactions upon issuance, whether received in loan or sale transactions,[192] under Section 7872, assuming that the note provides for adequate AFR interest, so that it does not represent a below-market loan.[193]

If the rule were otherwise, every intra-family loan (split-dollar or otherwise) would require a fair market, willing buyer–willing seller appraisal of the borrower's note and would result in a gift for federal gift tax purposes because a partially unsecured, potentially non-recourse term note with interest only at the AFR would, by definition, be worth less than face value if it were valued under a willing buyer–willing seller subjective standard.[194]

Under this objective valuation standard, a term note that provides for adequate AFR interest, issued by the borrower to the lender under a loan regime split-dollar arrangement (or as discussed in footnote 3, an intra-family sale transaction) would be valued at its face amount—equal to the amount loaned. Accordingly, it would be adequate and full consideration in money or money's worth for both federal gift and estate tax purposes and would therefore qualify the transaction for the exceptions to the application of Sections 2036(a)(2) and 2038(a)(1),[195] as well as for that exception to Section 2036(a)(1), as discussed later.[196]

In any event, as discussed later, because the lender in a loan transaction does not retain, either alone or in conjunction, with the trust, the power to terminate or accelerate the note (as opposed to a power to terminate the agreement, either under its terms or as provided by state law) and thereby determine who would benefit from the loan, nor the power to alter or amend the arrangement for purposes of Sections 2036(a)(2) or 2038(a)(1), by requiring the trust to transfer the policy to the lender in satisfaction of the note, the issue of the application of the exceptions under those provisions for transactions involving adequate and full consideration, described earlier, would never be relevant.

The argument is even stronger in a split-dollar loan regime arrangement because the lender that makes a term loan, as is always the case, whether in an intra-family loan or otherwise, has no right to terminate or accelerate the trust's term note, absent an uncured default. In fact, in a loan regime split-dollar transaction, there is no need to have a termination provision in the loan agreement at all, and unlike the common practice of including one in an economic benefit agreement, a split-dollar loan regime agreement wouldn't normally contain one.

However, even if a split-dollar loan regime agreement contained a mutual termination provision or if the parties had a mutual termination power under state law, which the parties exercised, termination of the agreement would not affect the trust's continued ownership of the policy nor the trust's obligation under the note. Because terminating the loan agreement would not accelerate the term of the note and would not therefore force the trust to transfer the policy to the lender in repayment of the note and thereby change which party owned the policy, the power to terminate the agreement (but not the note) can't be said to be a retained power to alter or amend the arrangement nor a retained power to designate the persons who will possess or enjoy the property or its income for purposes of Sections 2036(a)(2) nor 2038(a)(1).

3. *The Section 2036(a)(1) Issue*

In a split-dollar loan regime transaction, however, the IRS could argue that the lender had retained a right to income (the interest) from the transferred property (the amount loaned) under Section 2036(a)(1). The issue under

Section 2036(a)(1) therefore is whether the loan qualified for the adequate and full consideration exception to this section.

As noted earlier, the lender in a split-dollar loan regime transaction would not be treated as having made a gift to the borrower for federal gift tax purposes as a result of lending the initial premium on a policy to a trust in exchange for its term note because in addition to the application of the Section 7872 valuation rules to the loan when made, discussed earlier, under the IRS' rules applicable to split-dollar loan regime arrangements set forth in Treas. Reg. Sec. 1.7872-15, there is full consideration for the loan to the trust.[197] Accordingly, the arrangement would qualify as a transfer for "adequate and full consideration" under the exception to Section 2036(a)(1) and Treas. Reg. Sec. 20.2036-1.

See, for example, *Estate of Gertrude Friedman*,[198] *Wheeler v. US*,[199] and *Estate of Magnin v. Comm'r*,[200] which hold that if a transfer does not constitute a gift for gift tax purposes, it likewise cannot be considered as being a transfer for less than adequate and full consideration for estate tax purposes because the estate tax and gift tax are to be construed *in pari materia*. See also *Merrill v. Fahs*[201] and *Estate of Sanford v. Comm'r*,[202] to the same effect.

4. The Section 2073(a) Issue

In split-dollar loan regime transactions, there are no restrictions on the lender's ability to transfer, assign, or sell the note, either during lifetime or at death; the only possible restriction to which Section 2703(a) could apply in a loan regime transaction is the lender's inability to "use" the "property" owned at death—the note.[203] However, it is clear that the lender in a loan regime transaction can, without restriction, "use" the note by, among other things, selling it, gifting it, donating it, or using it as collateral for a loan during life or by bequeathing it at death. What other possible "use" of the note by the lender could be restricted under the terms of the note or the split-dollar loan agreement for Section 2703(a) purposes?

Does an inability to "call" a term loan note before maturity (absent a default) constitute a restriction on the holder's ability to "use" the note for Section 2703(a) purposes? If so, every intra-family loan represented by a term note would be subject to Section 2703(a) at the lender's death. In any event, this appears to be a restriction on the "use" of the amount loaned, not on the note itself.

The court in *Cahill—in dicta*—seems to have invited a distinction between receivables under economic benefit arrangements and notes under loan regime arrangements for Section 2703(a) purposes.

In its discussion of the application of Section 2703(a) to the economic benefit arrangements in *Cahill*, the court rejected the estate's argument that the receivables held by the decedent were similar to promissory notes because no interest was charged to "compensate" the lender for his loan. Its analysis of why the receivables were not similar to promissory notes suggests that promissory notes (presumably including those issued under a loan regime transaction) would be considered "bona fide notes" because they would compensate the lender for the loan with interest (in loan regime arrangements, at the AFR). In addition, if the representation required by the Final Split-Dollar Regulations for "non-recourse" loan regime notes,[204] that a "reasonable person" would expect the loans to be repaid, were made by the parties, it would, under these Regulations, treat the loans as "bona fide debt" for all federal tax purposes; they should then qualify as "bona fide notes" (in the words of the *Cahill* court) for purposes of Section 2703(a).

Finally, as discussed earlier, in a loan transaction, as opposed to an economic benefit transaction, there is no need to provide for terminating the loan agreement, either by the lender alone nor by the lender and borrower together because it is the provisions of the note that determine when the loan will be due and payable, not a provision in the loan agreement,[205] negating the existence of a restriction on the lender's ability to "use" the note for Section 2703(a) purposes.

5. *Conclusions as to the Application of the Sections 2036(a)(1), 2036(a)(2), and 2038(a)(1) Under These Cases to Loan Regime Transactions*

Neither Sections 2036(a)(2) nor 2038(a)(1) would apply to a split-dollar loan regime transaction to include any part of the value of the trust in the lender's estate for federal estate tax purposes because the lender would not possess the power, alone nor in conjunction with another, to alter or amend the arrangement nor to determine who would possess or enjoy the transferred property.

In addition because entering into a split-dollar loan regime transaction for a note that provided AFR interest does not result in a gift by the lender to the borrower for federal gift tax purposes, it therefore was for adequate and full consideration for the amount loaned, qualifying for the exceptions to each of those provisions and to Section 2036(a)(1).

6. *Conclusion as to the Application of Section 2703(a) Under These Cases to Loan Regime Transactions*

Section 2703(a) would not apply to value a note received in a split-dollar loan regime arrangement at anything other than its fair market value (under the usual willing buyer–willing seller standard) in the lender's estate for federal estate tax purposes because there are no restrictions on the lender's ability to sell or use the note, either during life or at death, which is the "property" to which Section 2703(a) would apply.

Because Section 2703(a) is inapplicable to the arrangement, whether the arrangement qualifies for the exceptions provided in Section 2703(b) is irrelevant.

7. *Summary of Conclusions*

In a split-dollar loan regime arrangement:

(1) Even if, in an usual situation, the decedent had retained the power with the trust to terminate the agreement or if that power was provided by state law, the power would not be either a Section 2036(a)(2) nor a 2038(a)(1) retained power because it would not terminate nor accelerate the note and would therefore not alter or amend the arrangement nor change who would benefit from the decedent's transfer. In addition, because of the trustee's fiduciary duty to the trust beneficiaries, the trustee could not have agreed to terminate the agreement and give up the policy; this restriction on the trustee's power to terminate the agreement would negate a retained power.

In any event, the decedent's AFR loan to the trust was for adequate and full consideration under the Section 7872 objective standard for valuing the trust's note on issuance, qualifying the transaction for the exceptions provided in Sections 2036(a)(1) and (2) and 2038(a)(1).

Finally, *Levine*'s rejection of the "gift on inception" concept would apply to prevent a gift on entering into the loan regime transaction, meaning there was no transfer for transfer tax purposes, so, in any event, neither Section 2036 nor 2038 could apply to the transaction.

(2) Section 2703(a) would not apply to value the note held at the decedent's death, which is the asset to which Section 2703(a) could have applied, at anything other than its fair market value, based on the usual willing buyer–willing seller concept because there would be no restrictions on the decedent's ability to sell or "use" the note, either during life or at death.

V. Economic Benefit Split-Dollar Arrangements

Unlike the premium financing loan arrangements, the premium payer (employer, corporation, service recipient, or donor) is the owner of the life insurance contract under an endorsement split-dollar arrangement. All or part of the pure death benefit is endorsed to the non-owner (employee, service provider, ILIT, or family member). Throughout this Part V, the terms "owner" and "non-owner" refer to these premium payers and endorsees, respectively.

The post-Final Split-Dollar Regulations economic benefit split-dollar regime is very similar to the old endorsement split-dollar regime under the pre-Regulations law, with similar income, employment, and gift tax consequences. These old endorsement split-dollar arrangements grandfathered from the Regulations are discussed later.

A. Non-equity Split-Dollar Exception to Ownership Rule

As discussed earlier, there is a major exception to the general rule of premium payer policy ownership for non-equity split-dollar arrangements. Even though the ILIT or the family member of the insured is the actual owner of the policy, the premium payer-employer, service provider, or donor is treated as being the owner for endorsement split-dollar purposes if the premium payer owns all of the policy cash value.[206] Note that this exception does not apply to corporation or shareholder split-dollar arrangements. This allows the ILIT or family member still to be the owner for estate tax incidents of ownership purposes under Section 2042, but the arrangement can still receive income and gift tax benefits from the endorsement economic benefit split-dollar rules.

However, certain modifications of the split-dollar contract could result in adverse tax consequences. If the non-equity split-dollar arrangement is modified (an undefined term) so that it ceases to be a non-equity split-dollar arrangement, if the employer, service recipient, or donor is no longer deemed to be the policy owner, then the employer, service provider, or donor is treated as having made a transfer of the entire life insurance contract to the employee, service provider, or donee as of the date of the modification.[207]

B. Reasons for Using Economic Benefit Split-Dollar Rather Than Premium Financing Loans

There are several potential reasons for the parties using economic benefit split-dollar rather than premium loans. First, the value of the annual economic benefit, as described later, to the non-owner endorsee (the employee, service provider, shareholder, ILIT, or family member) will be equal to the term premium on the endorsed pure death benefit. Until recently, this would have been a lower economic benefit than the AFR on the premium loan. In these days of very low AFRs, this might not be true except for insureds who are at an advanced age. If the lower economic benefit for income and gift purposes is the objective, the current AFR should be compared with the increasing term premium to see if the AFR might actually be lower.

A second reason is for the owner-employer, corporation, or donor to control the cash value of the policy. The owner will be able to invest the cash value if a variable life policy is involved and to prevent the endorsee from having access to the cash value. This might be important if the employer or corporation wants the equity cash value to provide a return on the premium investment. Also, the employer or corporation might want to use the cash value for its own purposes such as informally funding a nonqualified deferred compensation agreement with the insured employee or a redemption agreement for the stock of the shareholder.

In any event, as will be discussed later, the employer, corporation, or donor under the economic benefit split-dollar arrangement must own all of the cash value of the policy to prevent income and gift tax consequences if the endorsee has access to the cash value. Because the treatment of equity split-dollar arrangements is very unfavorable under the Final Split-Dollar Regulations, this regime is more useful for executive compensation than for wealth transfer. If it is intended for the employer, corporation, or donor to be paid off at a future date without surrendering the policy or stripping the cash value, an exit strategy will be required so that the endorsee will have the funds to purchase the cash value without untoward gift or income tax consequences—gifts, sales to a grantor trust, GRATs, CLATs, and so on as discussed earlier in this book.

C. What Are the Income and Gift Tax Consequences to the Non-owner of an Economic Benefit Split-Dollar Arrangement Under the Final Split-Dollar Regulations?

There are several possible economic benefits to the endorsee employee, service provider, shareholder, or donee under the Regulations, including the cost of current life insurance protection; current access to policy cash value (to extent not taxed in a prior year)l and all other economic benefits such as policy dividends, proceeds of specified policy loans, withdrawals, and partial surrenders (to the extent not taxed in a prior year) to the extent provided directly or indirectly to the endorsee non-owner. Most economic benefit split-dollar arrangements subject to the Final Split-Dollar Regulations limit the rights of the endorsee to all or part of the policy pure death benefit. Access to loans, dividends, withdrawals, and partial surrender proceeds is prohibited by the contract to avoid additional income and gift tax consequences. Accordingly, the economic benefit of the cost of current coverage is the most important issue, and it is discussed in detail later; the other economic benefits are also covered.

Any economic benefit from split-dollar arrangements is treated as provided from the owner to the non-owner.[208] The value of the economic benefit is reduced by any consideration paid by the non-owner. The tax treatment of the economic benefit depends on the relationship between the owner and the non-owner—employee or service provider (compensation), shareholder (dividend), or private split-dollar (gift). If a third party is involved, there could be two tax consequences (e.g., with regard to a split-dollar arrangement between an employer and an ILIT, compensation to the employee and gift by the employee to the ILIT).

It should also be noted in the economic benefit split-dollar arrangement that the non-owner will never receive any investment in the contract (basis) for the term premium for the cost of current insurance coverage whether reimbursed to the owner or included in the income of the non-owner.[209] The IRS position is that only a policy owner can accrue basis in a life insurance contract. The current cost of insurance coverage should not be included in the non-owner's basis if and when the non-owner becomes owner of the contract.[210] The Preamble states that this is because these payments were made for annual life insurance protection, and this protection was exhausted before the non-owner's acquisition of the contract.[211] However, if there is a rollout of the policy ownership to the non-owner upon termination of the split-dollar arrangement, the non-owner will receive basis at such time equal to any prior economic benefit included in gross income under current access to cash value and other amounts received under the contract.[212]

The amount of current life insurance protection and the policy cash value are determined on the last day of the non-owner's taxable year unless the owner and non-owner agree instead to use the policy anniversary date. However, if the economic benefit split-dollar arrangement terminates during the non-owner's taxable year, the valuation date is the date of termination. Both the owner and non-owner must use the same valuation date consistently for all years of the arrangement.[213] If an artifice or device is used to understate the amount of economic benefit on the valuation date, the amount of economic benefit is determined on the date that was the amount of the greatest economic benefit during the taxable year.[214]

1. Cost of Current Protection

This is the most significant economic benefit to the employee, service provider, shareholder, or donee under the economic benefit split-dollar arrangement. Current life insurance protection is the policy death benefit including paid up additions payable to the endorsee non-owner reduced by the total amount payable to the owner (usually the greater of premiums paid or policy cash value), which includes outstanding policy loans by the owner and reduced by any policy cash value taxable to the non-owner or paid for by the non-owner for the current or prior policy years. (e.g., current access cash value taxed to the non-owner, discussed later).[215] The annual cost of current life insurance, which is the economic benefit to the non-owner for income or gift tax purposes, equals the current insurance protection multiplied by term insurance premiums tables published in the *Internal Revenue Bulletin*.[216] This economic benefit is reduced by any premium paid by the non-owner.

The current term premium factors for a single life policy are set in Notice 2002-8.[217] Notice 2002-8 states that interim government Table 2001 (originally published in now revoked Notice 2001-10)[218] will be used to determine the cost of current insurance protection for a single life on or after January 28, 2002. Notice 2002-8 also provides that as an alternative to Table 2001, the taxpayer may use the insurer's lower published term rates that are available to all standard risks for initial issue term insurance if (1) the insurer generally makes the availability of such rates known to persons who apply for term insurance coverage from the insurer and (2) the insurer regularly sells term insurance at such rates to individuals who apply for term insurance coverage through the insurer's normal distribution channels. Because the carrier table must be available to all standard risks, neither non-smoker preferred rates[219] nor dividend option term rates for participating policies can be used.[220] If the insurer's table is only for corporate policies, it cannot be used for alternate split-dollar valuation.[221] The earlier two requirements were first added by Notice 2002-8, and as a result, many insurance companies have ceased publishing special split-dollar alternative tables. The

Service has reserved the right to change or abolish the use of the insurer's alternative term valuation table.

The carrier should be contacted to determine its position as to whether its term premium table qualifies or doesn't qualify under Notice 2002-8. Occasionally, a carrier shifts the burden of determining qualification to the policy owner based on facts supplied by the carrier.

With regard to valuing second-to-die policies, Notice 2002-8 states that the taxpayer "should make appropriate adjustments to these rates" but does not describe the adjustments. So what is the permitted adjustment? There is no guidance, but it is widely accepted practice to use the "revised US 38 Cost." This is based upon US 38 Cost used before Notice 2002-8 and still applicable to grandfathered split-dollar agreements entered into before January 22, 2002.

(a) Before 2002, because many insurance carriers did not market second-to-die term policies, the insurance industry widely used second-to-die term rates derived from then US Life Table 38, which involved multiplying the P.S. 58 Cost of one insured (a government term rate used before the much lower Table 2001 became effective) by the P.S. 58 Cost of the other insured with further multiplication by 1.025 as an adjustment for interest. This formula was often referred to as US 38 Cost and was contained in the "Greenberg to Greenberg" informational letter dated August 10, 1983.[222]

(b) There is no IRS or court authority endorsing US 38 Cost as the term value of a second-to-die policy. There is a private letter ruling in which the taxpayer used the "US Life Table 38" to measure the economic benefit for a second-to-die split-dollar arrangement.[223] However, the ruling did not address the US 38 Cost.

(c) Although the IRS has issued no guidance, many carriers use a revised US 38 Cost by substituting the lower Table 2001 rates for the revoked P.S. 58 Cost rates in the Greenberg to Greenberg letter formula. Since the revised US 38 Cost is based on the possibility of both insureds dying in the same year, they are dramatically lower that the Table 2001 rates for a single insured. If the carrier issues its own second-to-die term table it may be used as an alternative rate if the carrier's table meets the requirements of Notice 2002-8.[224] The author has been told that the revised US 38 Cost rate may be lower that the carrier's second-to-die table.

Note that when the first insured dies while the split-dollar arrangement is in existence, the much higher Table 2001 rates (or the carrier's lower single life term rate table) for the surviving insured will be the measure of the future economic benefit.[225] Advanced planning might make funds available at the first death to terminate the split-dollar arrangement and avoid the Table 2001 rates. If an ILIT is involved, the trustee could own single life policies on each insured sufficient to pay off the premium payer, or perhaps one or more of the exit strategies discussed earlier can be used to provide the funds. Some of the older second-to-die policies provided an increase in cash value at the first death which could be used but not for a non-equity split-dollar arrangement where the premium payer owns all of the cash value.

2. Current Access to Policy Values

As stated, most post-2003 economic benefit split-dollar arrangements limit the non-owner's rights in the policy to current insurance protection. The owner has all of the cash value and other rights in the policy. In such cases, the only economic benefit to the non-owner for income and gift tax purposes is the term cost of the current insurance protection.

However, if the non-owner also has current access to policy cash value, such accessible cash value is an additional economic benefit to the non-owner. An example is when the owner's rights in the policy are limited to the lesser of the aggregate premiums paid or the policy cash value. If the non-owner has current access to any equity cash value in excess of the owner's premium payments, such equity, unless already taxed in a prior year to the non-owner, will be an economic benefit for income and gift tax purposes.

(1) When is current access to cash value taxable? The answer is immediately. The Preamble to the Final Split-Dollar Regulations rejected the argument that cash value subject to current access be taxed under Section 83 at the date of rollout and transfer of such cash value to the non-owner. The current access cash value is currently taxable under Section 61 under doctrines such as constructive receipt, cash equivalence, or economic benefit.[226]

(2) What is current access? The non-owner has current access to any portion of the cash value to which the non-owner has a current or

future right (1) that currently is directly or indirectly accessible to the non-owner, (2) that is inaccessible to the owner, or (3) that is inaccessible to the owner's general creditors.[227] Note that even if the equity is not currently accessible by the non-owner, it is still an economic benefit if not accessible to either the owner or the owner's creditors. Also note that these three are in the disjunctive. Ironically, it would seem that if the non-owner cannot currently access the equity and state law prevents the owner's creditors from accessing it, the equity is taxable to the non-owner even though under state law or the terms of the policy the owner has full access to it. In states that deny access to the owner's creditors, it may be necessary for the split-dollar contract expressly to allow the creditors of the owner to reach the equity in the insurance policy to delay taxation of the equity to the non-owner. When is equity currently accessible by the non-owner? Equity cash value is currently accessible to the non-owner if the non-owner has any direct or indirect right under the arrangement allowing the non-owner to obtain, use, or realize potential economic benefit of the policy cash value equity. This includes the right to borrow or withdraw at any time the cash value in excess of the amount payable to the owner.[228] In addition, this includes the right to effect a total or partial surrender of the policy and to anticipate, assign, alienate, pledge, or encumber the policy cash value or if the equity cash value is available to the non-owner's creditors by attachment, garnishment, levy, execution, or other legal or equitable process.[229] In *Estate of Morrissette v. Comm'r*,[230] the IRS made an unsuccessful argument that the non-equity split-dollar arrangement between the grantor's revocable trust and the ILITs resulted in the ILITs' access to the policy cash values.[231] The Tax Court rejected the IRS argument that a provision in the revocable trust that its right to the greater of the premiums paid or cash value would be given to the ILITs or the ILITs' beneficiaries at the grantor's death was ILIT access to the cash value. The court noted that the revocable trust provisions did not give to the ILITs an enforceable right to the revocable trust's interest in policy cash values. Also, the court observed that there were no similar provisions in the split-dollar agreement giving these rights to the ILITs.[232]

(3) When is equity inaccessible to owner or owner's general creditors? Policy equity cash value is inaccessible to the owner if the owner does not have the full rights to policy cash value normally held by an owner in a life insurance contract. Equity policy cash value is

inaccessible to the owner's general creditors if, under the terms of the split-dollar arrangement or by operation of law or any contractual undertaking, the creditor cannot, for any reason, effectively reach the policy equity cash value in event of the owner's insolvency.[233] Some states restrict access to a policy and its cash value by the owner's creditors. Even if the non-owner is deemed to have current access to the cash value, the tax only appears when the equity appears (e.g., the spread between cash value and the premiums paid if the owner can only receive the lesser of the premiums or cash value).

3. *Other Amounts Received Under the Contract*

This is a catch-all economic benefit taxable to the non-owner—any amount received under a life insurance contract that is part of an economic benefit arrangement. This includes, but is not limited to, dividends, proceeds of a specified policy loan, withdrawals, or partial surrenders. To the extent these amounts are provided indirectly or directly to the non-owner, they will be treated as if paid to the owner and then paid to the non-owner by the owner. The distribution to the owner will be taxed pursuant to Section 72, and the payment to the non-owner will be taxable as income or a gift depending on the relationship between the owner and the non-owner.[234] Thus, if the non-owner employee withdraws $100,000 from the policy, the withdrawal will reduce the employer owner's basis under Section 72, and the non-owner will have cash compensation.[235]

The amount included in the non-owner's income or treated as a gift to the non-owner is equal to the excess of the amount received by the non-owner reduced by any amount taxed in a prior year as a current or prior year taxed current access cash value and consideration paid by the non-owner for such economic benefits.[236]

What is a specified policy loan that is an economic benefit to the non-owner? The regulations classify three alternative types of specified policy loans: (1) the proceeds of the loan are distributed directly from the insurance company to the non-owner, (2) a reasonable person would not expect the loan to be repaid by the non-owner, or (3) the non-owner's obligation to repay the loan to the owner is satisfied upon repayment by either party to the insurance company.[237] Thus, if the employee non-owner receives a specified policy loan of $100,000 directly from the insurance company, the $100,000 will be treated as a loan to the employer owner under Section 72 (such loan is not income and does not reduce the employer's investment in the contract) and as cash compensation paid by employer owner to the employee non-owner.[238] Any one of the three alternative types will create a taxable specified policy loan. However, not all loans benefitting a non-owner would be a specified policy loan. For example, it should be possible for an employer to use the proceeds of a policy loan to make a further loan to an employee without compensation

In the *Morrissette* case,[239] the IRS unsuccessfully argued that there were additional economic benefits. In an intergenerational split-dollar arrangement, the grantor's revocable trust paid a single lump sum premium for each policy owned by the ILITs with the anticipation that no more premiums would be due. The IRS argued that the prepaid premiums provided a benefit to the ILITs of future insurance protection and not just current insurance protection. The Tax Court rejected that argument on the grounds that the split-dollar contract required the grantor trust to pay all premiums. Thus, the prepayment of premiums did not relieve the ILITs of any premium obligation.

D. Are the Death Proceeds Payable to the Non-owner's Designated Beneficiary Taxable Under the Final Split-Dollar Regulations?

The death proceeds payable to a beneficiary (other than the owner) by reason of the death of the insured generally are excluded from the beneficiary's gross income under Section 101(a).[240] However, there are two possible exceptions to this rule under the Regulations.

(1) Under Treas. Reg. Sec. 1.61-22(e)(2), the Section 101(a) exclusion only applies to current life insurance protection–pure death proceeds over policy cash value. Thus, to the extent death proceeds include part of the pre-death cash value, the death benefit exclusion does not apply. However, the non-owner's basis in the cash value caused by taxation of the non-owner's current access to the equity cash value should offset the equity portion of the death proceeds to the beneficiary.

(2) A more serious problem is the Regulation requirement that the cost of "the current life insurance protection provided to the non-owner" is excluded if "the cost of which was paid by the non-owner, or the value of which the non-owner actually took into account."[241] In the Preamble to the Final Split-Dollar Regulations, the IRS rejected

comments that inclusion of current death benefits in the gross income of the beneficiary runs counter to exclusion under Section 101(a).[242] The Preamble further states that in situations when the non-owner neither pays nor includes in income the current life insurance protection, the proceeds are treated as if they were paid to the owner, excluded from the owner's income under Section 101(a) and distributed by the owner to the beneficiary outside of Section 101(a). The taxation of the deemed distribution depends on the relationship of the owner and non-owner—employer/executive (compensation), corporation/shareholder (dividend), or ILIT (gift).[243] Consequently, when the economic benefit split-dollar is in existence, it is important to have the non-owner executive scrupulously pay the term premium (which is not a good idea as explained later) or include it on the employee's W-2 to avoid an IRS argument that Section 101(a) does not apply. This is a serious penalty for lack of follow through, and some practitioners think this part of the Regulation may be invalid.

E. What Are the Income Tax Consequences to the Owner Under the Economic Benefit Final Split-Dollar Regulations?

(1) Reimbursement of term premium costs by the non-owner will be taxable to the owner. Any term or other economic benefit paid by the non-owner, directly or indirectly, to the owner of the life insurance contract is included in the owner's gross income.[244] This Regulation came as a surprise and is a change from the premium reimbursement rules for grandfathered split-dollar arrangements. The Preamble to the Regulation justifies the income inclusion of the term premium reimbursement on the grounds that the owner is "renting" out part of the insurance benefits to the non-owner for a consideration.[245] Presumably, there is no "indirect" reimbursement or income to the owner, employer, or corporation if the non-owner employee or shareholder does not pay the term premium but it is included in the employee's W-2 as compensation or in the shareholder's 1099 as a dividend. If the non-owner is the owner's grantor ILIT, the grantor trust rules of Revenue Ruling 85-13[246] will apply to disregard this income. In any event, most split-dollar arrangements after the Final Split-Dollar Regulations will not be reimbursement split-dollar arrangements.

(2) The owner's investment in the contract (basis) will include the premiums paid by the owner plus any term premium or other

economic benefit paid to the owner by the non-owner included in the owner's income (but only to the extent not otherwise so included by reason of having been paid by the owner as a premium or other consideration for the split-dollar contract).[247] Thus, the term premium paid by the non-owner will not constitute basis in the policy to the non-owner.[248]

(3) Any premium paid by the owner or employer under the split-dollar arrangement is not deductible by the employer.[249]

F. Impact of Transfer of an Economic Benefit Split-Dollar Contract from the Owner to the Non-owner

With regard to a split-dollar arrangement other than non-equity split-dollar, if the owner transfers the policy ownership or an undivided interest in the ownership to the non-owner, there are tax consequences.

The non-owner will take into account at the date of transfer for tax purposes the excess of fair market value of the life insurance contract (or undivided interest) over the amount paid by the non-owner for transfer and the value of any economic benefit received or paid for by the non-owner as prior current access to policy cash value or other amounts received under the contract (or undivided interest).[250] However, if the transfer is in connection with performance of services and is subject to a substantial risk of forfeiture, the policy transfer is taxable on the date it would be taxable under Section 83.[251] Note that the current cost of insurance coverage does not offset fair market value. Thus, such excess fair market value would be compensation or dividend to an employee or stockholder non-owner, respectively.[252] The excess will be a gift from the owner donor to the non-owner donee.

What is the "fair market" value of the contract?

1. Non-gift Transfers

For transfers that are not a gift between a donor owner and a donee non-owner, the fair market value is the "policy cash value and the value of all other rights under the contract (including any supplemental agreements thereto and whether or not guaranteed)."[253] Note that there is no mention of reduction for surrender charges, and this appears to be deliberate. The proposed split-dollar regulation stated that fair market value was "the cash surrender value," but the word "surrender" was deleted in the Final Split-Dollar Regulations without comment. This conclusion is reinforced by a 2003 contemporaneous amendment to the Section 83 regulation,[254] which provided, for Section 83 property transfer purposes, that a life insurance contract is valued at "policy cash value and all other rights under the contract (including any supplemental agreements thereto whether or not guaranteed)" but that contracts grandfathered from the Final Split-Dollar Regulations are valued at "only the cash surrender value." Also note that the Final Split-Dollar Regulations' definition of cash value for current access economic benefit "is determined disregarding surrender charge or other similar charges or reductions."[255] Thus surrender charges almost certainly are ignored in determining fair market value policy cash value.

Fair market value is not just "policy cash value" but also includes "all other rights under the contract (including any supplemental agreements thereto, and whether or not guaranteed)." The quoted language is not defined by the Regulation. In the routine split-dollar policy, could these "other rights" significantly increase the policy fair market value? The identical language was added in the 2004 Section 83 regulation amendment to the value of life insurance contract, including split-dollar arrangements.[256] The term is not defined in the Section 83 regulation either. However, Rev. Proc. 2005-25[257] gives guidance for determining fair market value for transfers of policies from qualified plans and for group term policies with permanent benefits under Section 83. The Revenue Procedure makes it clear that the fair market value rules apply to the cash value and other rights definition in the Section 83 regulations. The Revenue Procedure goes on to create separate safe harbor formulas for valuing non-variable and variable policies—greater of interpolated terminable reserve and any unearned premiums plus pro rata portion of reasonable dividends for the year or the sum of premiums, earnings, and reasonable charges (PERC) over the prior term of the policy. Such a calculation may or may not have any relationship to policy cash value. "Interpolated terminable reserve" is used to establish fair market value for gift tax purposes.

Does this mean that the gift tax valuation using interpolated terminable reserve also is used (with the PERC adjustment) rather than "policy cash value" for split-dollar transfer under the Final Split-Dollar Regulations? Maybe not because the Regulations also state that "notwithstanding the preceding sentence, the fair market value of a contract for gift tax purposes is determined under Treas. Reg. Sec. 25.2512-6(a)."[258] That strongly implies that the gift tax valuation rules do not apply to compensation nor dividend split-dollar arrangements.

If the IRS does mean policy cash value (with minor adjustments for other economic rights) is the measure of fair market value for transfer to an employee or shareholder non-owner, how would this apply to no lapse guarantee policies that have little or no cash value but the insurance has significant deficiency or other reserves to back up the death benefit guarantee? This may be an instance when the "other rights" or "supplemental agreements" may result in a fair market value well in excess of cash value.

Policy cash value fair market value might be attacked by the IRS if the cash value is kept artificially low and total policy reserves are substantially higher. This would be similar to the IRS argument in Notice 89-25[259] concerning "springing" cash values of policies distributed from qualified plans. In that notice, the IRS asserted that the policy reserves represented a more accurate approximation of fair market value than depressed cash surrender value. The qualified plan regulations were amended in 2004 to replace cash value with fair market value.[260] Although split-dollar arrangements with employee or shareholder non-owner is valued at policy cash value ignoring surrender charges, the philosophy behind Notice 89-25 might still apply if the cash value is substantially below policy reserves by some other means.

Another analogy that low cash value might be replaced by higher policy reserves may be found in the Section 72 regulation, which provides that the cash value portion of death proceeds from a policy owned by a qualified plan is includible in the beneficiary's gross income and only the pure death benefit is excluded under Section 101(a).[261] The regulation states that the insurance carriers "reserve accumulation constitutes the source of the cash value of the contract and approximates the amount of the cash value." So, if the policy reserves substantially exceed the policy cash value, the implication is that the reserves are the measure of gross income.

2. *Gift Transfers*

For transfers that are a gift between a donor owner and a donee non-owner, the fair market value of a life insurance contract for gift tax purposes is determined under Treas. Reg. Sec. 25.2512-6(a).[262] Instead of using policy cash value, the gift tax regulation states that the value is established by "the sale of the particular contract by the company, or through the sale by the company of comparable contracts." The regulation observes that a sale of a comparable contract may not be readily ascertainable when the gifted contract has been in force for some time and on which further premium payments are to be made. In such a case, the "value may be approximated by adding to the interpolated terminal reserve at the date of the gift the proportionate part of the gross premium last paid before the date of the gift which covers the period extending beyond that date."[263] In short, the value of an existing split-dollar policy with more premiums to pay is interpolated terminal reserve plus unused premium.

If the split-dollar policy is a single premium or otherwise paid up policy with no more premiums to pay,[264] the fair market value is the amount the carrier would charge for a single premium contract of the same specified coverage on the life of a person of the current age of the insured.[265] Under the analogous estate tax value of a single premium policy, when the premium paid on a comparable single premium policy would have purchased a replacement policy with cash value below the cash value of the single premium policy being valued, the IRS used interpolated terminal reserve plus unused premium.[266]

The concept of interpolated terminal reserve does not fit well with universal or variable life policies that came out after the regulation. A non-variable whole life policy has a known reserve at the next anniversary date from which to interpolate. However, the reserve at the next anniversary date for a universal or variable life policy will not be known until that date, and several different reserves could be used.

What is the reserve for a universal or variable life policy? There is no guidance from the IRS. Some insurers use statutory reserves required by state law, and others use tax reserves that determine the carrier's federal income tax—with widely varying results. Because there is no guidance, some carriers report the value as cash value, accumulation value or average of cash, and accumulation values. A few carriers list two or three of the these reserve valuations on their IRS Forms 712 and leave the decision up to the taxpayers and their attorneys to choose the correct value.

No lapse guarantee universal policies cause more perplexing valuation issues. These policies have increased reserves because there is a valuable guaranteed death benefit with little or no cash value. The National Association of Insurance Commissioners (NAIC) established Actuarial Guidelines 38 Reserve (the "AG 38 Reserve") in 2003 to apply to the statutory and tax reserves to reflect the additional no lapse guarantee value. The AG 38 Reserve has been modified upward by NAIC in 2005, 2007, and 2013.

Some carriers add a deficiency reserve in addition to the AG 38 Reserve. In 2001, NAIC issued a UL Model Regulation to calculate the reserves for traditional universal life policies. In that calculation, there is an alternative minimum reserve. If that alternative minimum reserve exceeds the UL Model Regulation Reserve or the AG 38 Reserve, some carriers create a deficiency reserve for such excess. The reserve entered by the carrier on Form 712 may reflect the AG 38 Reserve and maybe the additional deficiency reserve.

Before requesting a Form 712 on a large policy, the taxpayer may want to contact the carrier's underwriters to find out what reserve valuation is being used to avoid surprises, or the taxpayer might request a Form 712 before the transfer to check out the carrier's valuation early. However, Form 712 must be attached to IRS Forms 706 and 709, and if the taxpayer uses a different reserve valuation from that used by the carrier on Form 712, the taxpayer should attach an explanation or a separate appraisal.

Even if the interpolated terminable reserve value has been determined, it still might not be the value of the transferred split-dollar policy under the gift tax regulation. The regulation states "if, however, because of unusual nature of the contracts such approximation [sale of comparable contracts] is not reasonably close to the full value, this method may not be used."[267] In other words, the examples in the gift tax regulations are only rules of thumb that may be trumped by other facts.

So what is the unusual nature of the contract that affects policy fair market value? A major factor is the fact that the insured's health is seriously impaired at the time of transfer. In a Tax Court case, the insured on his death bed sold his insurance contracts to his daughter for cash surrender value.[268] The Tax Court determined that the policies were worth considerably more than the cash value at the date of sale, stating that: "The investment value of life insurance . . . is greatly affected by the life expectancy of the insured, and the value rises in inverse ratio to the length of that life expectancy."[269]

Would the value be increased if the insured is not on his death bed but his health is seriously impaired? The *Pritchard* case mentions that value is greatly affected by a shortened life expectancy even though death was imminent in that case. A private letter ruling ruled that the value of a second-to-die policy was interpolated terminal reserve plus unused premiums when the insureds "were not in danger of imminent death, nor did they have medical problems that would unexpectedly shorten their life expectancy. . . ."[270]

What if the split-dollar policy is eligible for sale on the life settlement market at the date of transfer? Would this be an unusual nature of the contract? The life settlement market is generally available for large policies on the lives of insureds with impaired health but not necessarily a markedly reduced life expectancy. Generally, the market looks for an insured older than 65 years of age with poor health for a policy with small cash value. The purchase price would be higher than cash value. Would not a life settlement policy more closely meet the willing buyer–seller test than the sale of a comparable policy? The IRS has not yet gone as far as to argue life settlement value for gift tax purposes in the appropriate case. Form 712 only lists interpolated terminal reserve plus unused premium or replacement premium for a single premium policy. Because the policy is being transferred by donor owner to non-owner donee, the parties probably do not know a life settlement might be available.

G. Impact of Modifying the Ownership of a Non-equity Split-Dollar Arrangement

In non-equity economic benefit split-dollar arrangements, the premium payer is "treated" as the policy owner for tax purposes even though the other party actually owns the policy for contractual purposes. This allows the arrangement to fall under the economic benefit regime. When the premium payer is the real owner, the earlier discussion presents the tax consequences of the real owner transferring the policy. With regard to the non-equity split-dollar arrangement, what if the premium payer transferred the payer's non-equity interest to the other party so that the split-dollar arrangement ends? There is no actual transfer of the policy by the premium payer because the other party was already the contractual owner of the policy. The tax rules already discussed for transfer of the entire policy to the non-owner literally do not apply.

The IRS attempted to close this potential tax loophole in the Final Split-Dollar Regulations.[271] The Regulations first provide that if the arrangement is modified to not qualify as a non-equity split-dollar arrangement but the premium payer-employer, service recipient, or donor becomes the actual owner of the policy, then the split-dollar economic benefit rules continue to apply (e.g., premium payer becomes actual owner and the employee, service provider or donee becomes the endorsee of the pure death benefit).[272]

The Regulations next provide that if the non-equity exception applies and if the arrangement is "modified" so as not to qualify for the non-equity exception (e.g., part of the cash value is made available to the employee, service provider, or donee) and immediately after the modification the employer, service recipient, or donor premium payer is no longer treated as the owner under the split-dollar arrangement, the premium payer "is treated as having made a transfer of the entire life insurance contract to the employee, service provider or donee" for income and/or gift tax purposes under the rules of Regulation Section 1.61-22(g) discussed earlier.

What is a "modification"? It is not defined by the regulation, but clearly, a transfer of part of the cash value to the former non-owner would be because the policy would no longer qualify as non-equity. Presumably, a sale or gift of the premium payer's entire interest in the policy to the employee, service provider, or donee would be a modification because it also changes the economic benefit of the arrangement. However, there is another school of thought that a gift or sale of the premium payer's entire interest in the policy is not a modification but a termination of the arrangement avoiding the Final Split-Dollar Regulations. According to this argument, a modification only involves a change in the non-equity rights of the premium payer who would still retain rights to some of the cash value.

This is an important distinction when an intergenerational discount arrangement is involved. Under a typical discount split-dollar arrangement, an ILIT for the benefit of a grandchild owns a policy on the life of the child. Pursuant to a non-equity private split-dollar arrangement, the grandparent assumes an obligation to pay the premiums in excess of the ILIT's term premium for the pure death benefit coverage with no right to terminate the arrangement or to access the cash value. After a few years, the grandparent sells or gives ownership of the cash value to the ILIT, terminating the split-dollar arrangement. Because the cash value is tied up until the death of the child, the goal is to take a large discount for the cash value sale or gift. If the sale or gift is not a modification, then arguably, the value of the gift or sale of the premium payer's interest is discounted under the restrictions of the split-dollar arrangement. On the other hand, if the sale or gift is a modification, then the value of the premium payer's interest is its fair market value under the Final Split-Dollar Regulations and not the discounted value. Is a termination also a modification? It might be the ultimate modification, but there are no authorities on point. In addition to the termination or modification issue, there are many other uncertainties involving discount split-dollar for which there are no authorities.[273] However, the IRS has not raised this issue during several recent audits; instead, the IRS has attacked the size of the discount. We understand that there have been several settlements of this valuation issue very favorable to the taxpayer.

As noted earlier, in the recent *Morrissette* case,[274] the IRS took the position that a near $30 million lump sum premium payment, pursuant to a non-equity intergenerational split-dollar arrangement, was a gift from the grantor's revocable trust to dynasty ILITs owning policies on the lives of the grantor's sons. The arrangement was designed to give the ILITs funds to purchase from a deceased insured son's estate the stock he owned in a family company. One of the IRS arguments was that the arrangement was a zero interest loan regime and not an non-equity economic benefit regime. The Tax Court rejected the IRS contention that the ILITs had benefits other than current insurance protection—access to policy cash value because the revocable trust was paid to the ILIT at the grantor's death and that the prepayment of premiums was an economic benefit to the ILITs.[275]

H. Switch Dollar

This is a split-dollar policy that starts under the endorsement split-dollar regime. It later ends the endorsement and "switches" to premium financing under the loan regime. This technique was more popular in the days when the AFR was well above the historic low rates since November 2008 when the mid-term annual AFR dropped below 3%.[276]

In those times, the AFR was likely to be higher than the term premium for the pure death benefit on the life of the insured unless the insured was an older adult. It would make sense to have an economic benefit split-dollar in which the term premium to be included in income or treated as a gift likely is less than the AFR. The problem with continuing the economic benefit split-dollar is that when cash value exceeds the aggregate premiums, the premium payer owner will own this equity cash value and not the employee, service provider, or donee non-owner.

The solution is "switch dollar." At the point where the cash value of the policy equals the aggregate premiums, the economic benefit split-dollar arrangement is terminated and "switched" to a loan regime by treating the employee, service provider, or donee as the policy owner with an execution of a promissory note in favor of the premium payer equal to the greater of the cash value and the aggregate premiums at the date of the switch. Even if the termination were considered a modification, the fair market value of the policy that was treated as transferred should be totally or significantly offset by the value of the promissory note.

The effect is that the lower term premium is used until the switch with an AFR interest rate used after the switch. If the switch is just before the appearance of cash value equity or if the arrangement had been non-equity, no cash value should be taxed, and the new owner will benefit from future accrual of cash value tax free. As noted earlier, the termination of the economic benefit arrangement by repaying the premium provider with a note should not be considered a modification subject to the Regulation provision. But in these days of very low interest rates, it may well be that the AFR is lower than the term rate. If so, the loan regime should be used from the beginning.

Caveat: The deemed transfer of ownership in the switch could be considered a transfer for value of the policy, although it would seem that would require an *actual,* not a *deemed,* transfer. If so, if it were treated as a transfer for value, it would be important that the owner after the switch be a person exempt from the transfer for value rules that would otherwise make the policy death proceeds included in the beneficiary's gross income (the insured, a partner of the insured, a partnership in which the insured is a partner, and so on),[277] or the deemed transfer should qualify for the carry-over basis exemption from those rules (as a deemed transfer between the donor-insured and a grantor trust would be).

I. Gift and Estate Tax Consequences of Economic Benefit Split-Dollar Arrangements

1. Gift Taxes

This occurs in a wealth transfer context when someone other than the insured is the non-owner (e.g., a family member or an ILIT). Because the ILIT is the usual non-owner, this discussion will concentrate on split-dollar arrangements with ILITs, although the gift tax consequences with other non-owners should be approximately the same. Most of this discussion can be found elsewhere in this Part V combined with income taxes, but it is consolidated here in one place for gift taxes.

With regard to a private split-dollar arrangement between the insured donor and the ILIT, all economic benefits provided by the donor will be a taxable gift. If it is a non-equity arrangement in which the donor or the donor's estate is entitled to the greater of cash value or premiums paid, the gift is the term premium for current cost of insurance less premiums paid by the trustee.[278] Furthermore, if the ILIT has current access to policy cash value (e.g., the donor is entitled to the lesser of cash value and premiums paid), then the cash value subject to such access (to the extent not already a gift in a prior year) in addition to the current cost of life insurance protection will be the amount of the taxable gift. Likewise, if the ILIT is entitled to other economic benefits (e.g., dividends, specified loans, withdrawals, or partial surrenders), these benefits will also be taxable gifts to the extent not a gift in a prior year and added to the other above economic benefits.[279] These taxable gifts are reduced by all premiums paid by the ILIT trustee that could totally offset the gift.[280] In short, the economic benefits that would be compensation to the non-owner employee in a compensatory economic benefit split-dollar arrangement is the taxable gift in a private economic benefit split-dollar arrangement.[281]

A compensatory split-dollar arrangement may result in taxable gifts if the owner-employer or corporation enters into an economic benefit split-dollar arrangement with the employee's or shareholder's ILIT. In such a situation because the employer or corporation is entering into the arrangement because of relationship to the employee or shareholder, the regulation treats the arrangement as two steps—a compensatory transfer of economic benefits to the employee or shareholder and a gift from the employee or shareholder to the ILIT.[282]

If an interest in an economic benefit split-dollar policy is given away to an ILIT, there will be a taxable gift of that interest in the policy. There are two gift scenarios with slightly different results.

(a) Gift by the non-owner to a third party, such as an ILIT. The split-dollar arrangement continues after the gift between the owner and the new non-owner ILIT. The value of the gift is the value of the policy under the gift tax regulations reduced by the owner's interest in the policy. For example, if the non-owner employee gives the employee's interest in the policy to the employee's child, the IRS has ruled that the value of an existing policy with more premiums to be paid is the interpolated terminal reserve plus unused premiums reduced by the employer's interest in the policy.[283] Even though the 1981 revenue ruling predated the Final Split-Dollar Regulations, the Preamble to the Final Split-Dollar Regulations states that the "gift tax consequences of the transfer of an interest in a life insurance contract to a third party will continue to be determined under established gift tax principles notwithstanding who is treated as owner of the life insurance contract under the final regulation."[284] The Preamble cites the 1981 revenue ruling. Thus, the valuation of the gift is the same whether or not a grandfathered endorsement split-dollar arrangement (or a loan regime, for that matter) is involved. However, the fair market value and how to calculate interpolated terminal reserve issues discussed earlier in Part V of this book are pertinent.

(b) Gift by a donor owner to donee non-owner by modification of non-equity split-dollar arrangement. This is a gift wherein a modification of the split-dollar arrangement ends the non-equity split-dollar rule that treats the premium payer as the donor-owner even though the donee non-owner actually owns the policy. The modification is treated as a gift of the entire policy to the non-owner with fair market value of the gift being determined under the gift tax regulation reduced by any consideration paid by the non-owner.[285]

2. *Estate Taxes*

The Preamble to the Final Split-Dollar Regulations states that Section 2042 applies to split-dollar policies regardless of who is the owner if payable to the insured's estate or if the insured possessed incidents of ownership in the policy at death (or within 3 years before death if Section 2035 applies). However, in the Regulations, the IRS declined to "address the extent to which a decedent's interest in a co-owned policy is includible in the decedent's gross estate under Section 2042."[286]

If the economic benefit split-dollar arrangement is compensatory and has the insured as the non-owner, then the death benefit less the employer's interest in the policy (deductible as a debt owed by the estate to the employer) will be included in the employee's gross estate because the insured employee possessed incidents of ownership.[287] On the other hand, in a private split-dollar arrangement in which the insured possessed incidents of ownership, all of the death proceeds, including the amount payable to the donee ILIT, will be included in the insured donor's gross estate.[288]

After the Final Split-Dollar Regulations, an economic benefit split-dollar arrangement requires the premium payer to be the owner. But in a private split-dollar arrangement (e.g., insured donor or ILIT), if the insured is the owner, the insured would have incidents of ownership. As discussed earlier, under the non-equity split-dollar exception, the insured donor premium payer will be treated as the owner for income and gift tax purposes but not for estate taxes because the donee ILIT is the actual owner.[289] The IRS has blessed this arrangement in at least two private letter rulings.[290]

There is another potential incident of ownership problem if the donor insured has a security interest in the policy—a collateral assignment against the policy to protect the donor's interest even though a loan is not involved. The typical collateral assignment gives the premium payer the power, in order to receive the premium payer's investment in the policy, to withdraw or borrow from the cash value or even surrender the policy. These would be incidents of ownership even though the ILIT owns the policy. To avoid an incident of ownership argument, the IRS has approved split-dollar arrangements with the insured possessing a restricted access or "bare bones" assignment in which all of the incidents of ownership belong to the ILIT, and the insured's only right is to be paid at termination of the arrangement.[291]

There is also a potential incident of ownership problem if there is an economic benefit split-dollar arrangement between the insured's controlled corporation and the ILIT. Under the estate tax regulation, the incidents of ownership, owned by a corporation on the life of more than 50% shareholder, in death proceeds payable to someone other than the controlled corporation or for a valid business purpose of the corporation will be attributable to the insured.[292] Thus, if the controlled corporation receives death proceeds equal to the greater of policy cash value immediately before death and aggregated premiums paid, these death proceeds will not be included in the insured's gross estate.[293] The death proceeds payable to the ILIT will be included in the insured's gross estate. As in the case of the private non-equity split-dollar arrangements, if the ILIT owns the policy but the economic benefit regime applies because the split-dollar arraignment is drafted as a non-equity arrangement, the controlled corporation has no incidents of ownership to attribute to the insured shareholder. If a collateral assignment in favor of the controlled corporation is used, be sure it is a restricted access or "bare bones" assignment to avoid imputation of incidents of ownership to the insured-controlling shareholder. There are several private letter rulings to this effect.[294] Although they predate the Final Split-Dollar Regulations, these rulings should still be instructive for economic benefit split-dollar arrangements subject to the Regulations.

What are the estate tax issues if the economic benefit split-dollar arrangement is between a partnership and a partner's ILIT involving a policy on the partner's life? The Final Split-Dollar Regulations do not discuss partnership split-dollar. The Regulation has a provision entitled "life insurance contracts owned by partnerships" indicating the subject is "reserved."[295] The same income, gift, and estate tax rules should apply to partnership split-dollar arrangement as to other types of split-dollar arrangements subject to any peculiar rules relating to partnerships. However, the attribution of partnership incidents of ownership to the insured partner may depend on whether the partnership is deemed to be an aggregation of all partners ("aggregate theory") or a separate entity for estate tax purposes ("entity theory"). There is no regulation for partnership incidents of ownership as there is for more than 50% controlled corporations.

a. Aggregate Theory

The partnership is considered an aggregate of its partners. Thus, any incidents of ownership in a policy on the life of a partner is deemed owned by the insured partners. The IRS has adopted the aggregate theory for partnerships in Rev. Rul. 83-147.[296] Although a split-dollar policy was not involved in the ruling, the partnership owned a policy on the life of a one-third partner. At the partner's death, two-thirds of the death proceeds were paid to the partner's child and one-third to the partnership. The IRS expressly ruled that a partnership was an aggregate entity and that incidents of ownership were attributable to the insured partner but that only the proceeds paid to the child would be included in the partner's gross estate. The one-third payable to the partnership was not includible in the gross estate because the proceeds would increase the value of the insured partner's partnership interest. Thus, direct inclusion of that one-third in the partner's gross estate under Section 2042(2) would result in unwarranted double taxation.

There are several things to note from the ruling. First, the attribution of incidents of ownership applied even though the insured partner was not a majority partner as would have been required for a controlled corporation. Presumably, a 1% partnership interest would trigger inclusion. Second, the partnership has to possess incidents of ownership in order to have attribution. In Ltr. Rul. 9204041, the partnership's interest in the split-dollar arrangement with an ILIT was subject to a restricted access bare bones collateral assignment. The IRS ruled that the partnership did not have incidents of ownership. Although a split-dollar policy was not involved, the IRS has ruled that an insured partner has no incidents of ownership in a policy owned by the partnership in which the partnership agreement prohibited an insured partner from exercising an incident of ownership for a policy on the partner's life.[297] Likewise, when a partnership owned a policy on the life of a limited partner, the IRS ruled that there are no incidents of ownership in the limited partner because the management control was limited to the general partner.[298]

Suppose the split-dollar insurance proceeds payable to the partnership would not increase the value of the insured's partnership interest (e.g., a buyout contract that excludes key person insurance proceeds from being included in the value of the insured's partnership interest). Perhaps, in this case, the death proceeds payable to the partnership might also be includible in the insured partner's gross estate with the share paid to the ILIT because there would not be any "unwarranted double taxation."

b. Entity Theory

Under this theory, the partnership is a separate entity, and any incidents of ownership in policies on lives of partners are never attributable to the insured partner unless the partnership vale is pierced as a sham. It would be treated as a separate entity like a corporation. The only reason the incidents of ownership owned by a corporation on the life of its controlling shareholder are included in the shareholder's gross estate is because there is a regulation so stating.[299]

A partnership is a pass-through entity for income taxes, but is it for estate tax purposes? Arguably, the Tax Court has adopted the entity theory.[300] In the *Knipp* case, the partnership owned policies on a partner's life that were payable to the partnership. The Tax Court held no attribution of incidents of ownership to the insured partner, not because the proceeds were payable to the partnership but because "the insurance was an asset of the partnership and Frank had no rights in the policy other than those flowing from his partnership interest."[301] The IRS acquiesced in result only because the proceeds were paid to the partnership. The IRS General Counsel expressed concern that the Tax Court had adopted the entity theory with the result that incidents of ownership would never be attributed to an insured partner.[302] Undaunted, the Tax Court reached the same conclusion as in *Knipp* in *Watson v. Commissioner*.[303] *Knipp* and *Watson* both involved 50% partners. Would their decision be the same if the insured partner owned more than 50%? Presumably, yes because there is no controlled partnership regulation like there is for a controlled corporation. However, *Knipp* implies that it was leaving the over 50% situation to another day.[304]

In summary, rather than fight with the IRS as to whether the entity theory applies, avoid the issue by depriving the partnership of any incidents of ownership under a bare bones collateral assignment or by having the partnership agreement deny an insured partner the power to exercise incidents of ownership in policies on his life owned by the partnership.

J. Intergenerational Private Split-Dollar Arrangements

1. Example

A grandparent establishes an ILIT in favor of his or her grandchildren. The trust purchases an insurance policy on the life of the grandparent's child. The premium of the policy is financed by a collateral assignment non-equity split-dollar arrangement between the trust and the grandparent that would be subject to the economic benefit regime. The premium payments under the arrangement are front-end loaded, often in a single premium, but sometimes in a few premiums to avoid the MEC rules. The split-dollar arrangement prevents the grandparent from terminating the arrangement. The grandparent will be entitled to the greater of the premium payments or policy cash value at the termination the split-dollar contract, cancellation of the policy, or the death of the insured.

2. Split-Dollar Contract Restrictions Discount

For estate tax valuation purposes, proponents argue that the greater of the premium payments of the policy cash value is reduced by the restrictive split-dollar contract as determined by actuarial appraisal. Such a contract would normally prevent reimbursement or cash value until the death of the insured child, and the grandparent would not be given a right to terminate the split-dollar agreement. Proponents argue that the present value of the split-dollar contract in the grandparent's estate is severely reduced by the grandparent being unable to terminate the arrangement until the death of the insured child.

3. Estate Levine v. Commissioner[305]

After two false starts, taxpayers had a big win in the *Levine* case. This decision by the full Tax Court blessed the discount evaluation of a split-dollar agreement if certain requirements are met. The following is a brief summary of the facts.

Mrs. Levine had a real estate empire worth more than $25 million.

Years ago, Levine placed most of her assets into a revocable trust with her son; daughter; and Robert Larson, a close business friend and controller of the family business, as co-trustees.

Upon Levine's death, irrevocable trusts were created for the son, daughter, and grandchildren.

A joint power of attorney was given to the son, daughter, and Larson in 2005. They used the power to create an ILIT in 2008. The son, daughter, and grandchildren were beneficiaries. A corporate trust company was the directed trustee with Larson being the investment trustee.

The ILIT bought two whole life second-to-die insurance policies on the lives of the daughter and her husband. (The son was rated for insurability purposes.)

A total of $6.5 million was contributed to the ILIT by the revocable trust (which it received from loans from third parties and from family businesses by the son, daughter, and Larson pursuant to the power of attorney and in their capacities as trustees of the revocable trust) to provide for the payment of a lump sum premium pursuant to a split-dollar agreement executed by the revocable trustees and the agents under the power of attorney. The major terms of the split-dollar agreement were as follows:

(1) The Levine revocable trust would receive the greater of the premiums paid or the cash value of the policies upon the termination of the split-dollar agreement, the surrender of the insurance policies, or the death of the survivor of the insureds.

(2) Larson as the investment trustee had the sole power to terminate the split-dollar agreement or surrender the insurance policies. Levine and her revocable trust had no power to terminate the split-dollar agreement.

(3) All incidents of ownership in the insurance policies were retained by the trustees of the ILIT.

Mrs. Levine's mental capacity began to decline significantly in 2008, and she died in 2009.

At Levine's death, the cash value of the insurance policies was $6,153,478. Based on a discount for a non-equity split-dollar agreement under the economic benefit regime, the estate claimed the value of the split-dollar agreement was $2 million. The estate and the IRS stipulated that the discounted value was $2,282,195 if the estate prevailed. However, the IRS claimed that the entire cash value was includible in Levine's estate pursuant to IRC Sections 2036, 2038, and 2703. The unanimous Tax Court ruled in favor of the taxpayer.

4. *Sections 2036 and 2038*

Section 2036 includes in the decedent's estate the value of property decedent transferred during lifetime if, after the transfer, the decedent kept either possession or the right to income from the property or even if the decedent kept a right (either alone or in connection with another) to designate who would receive possession of the property or its income.

Section 2038 includes in the decedent's estate the value of property that the decedent transferred during lifetime in which the decedent retained an interest or right (either alone or in conjunction with another) to alter, amend, revoke, or terminate the transferee's enjoyment of the transferred property.

The Levine Tax Court concluded that the property transferred was not the insurance policies (they were bought and owned by the ILIT) but the right under the split-dollar agreement to receive the greater of cash value or $6.5 million premium payments upon termination of the split-dollar agreement. Sections 2036 and 2038 do not apply because only Larson as co-trustee could terminate the split-dollar agreement, and Levine and her trust could not.

In the *Estate of Cahill v. Commissioner*,[306] the Tax Court concluded that a split-dollar contract provision that allowed the ILIT and the owner of the split-dollar agreement to mutually terminate the contact was a retained right bringing Sections 2036 and 2038 into play. Cahill had the right, in conjunction with the ILIT trustee, to terminate the agreement. The Tax Court reached the same conclusion in *Estate of Morrissette v. Commissioner* by order dated February 19, 2019.

The Levine Tax Court rejected the IRS argument that Sections 2036 and 2038 should apply because general contract law gives the parties the power to jointly modify any contract. It concluded that Sections 2036 and 2038 only apply to rights to terminate created in the split-dollar contract and not to general default rules of contract.

The Levine Tax Court also rejected the IRS argument that Levine, through her attorneys, in fact stood on both sides of the split-dollar agreement and therefore could unwind it at any time, thereby subjecting it to Sections 2036 and 2038. The Court pointed out that only Larson was on both sides of the transaction as an attorney in fact and as a co-trustee. Although he represented Mrs. Levine as an attorney-in-fact, he was a co-trustee along with the bank of the ILIT. Larson had fiduciary duties under state law and could not terminate the split-dollar agreement to benefit the son and daughter without taking into consideration his fiduciary duties to the grandchildren, who were also beneficiaries of the ILIT.

Unlike Levin, what if a court determined that Sections 2036 and 2038 did apply? There is an exception under both sections if the split-dollar agreement involves a transfer, which is a bona fide sale for adequate and full consideration. To meet this exception, the taxpayer must have a legitimate and significant non-tax purpose and receive adequate and full consideration for money or money's worth.

The taxpayer in *Estate of Morrissette v. Commissioner*[307] met this exception (although lost in the valuation of the split-dollar agreement discussed later). In *Morrissette*, with regard to significant non-tax reasoning the ILIT and split-dollar agreement were tied to a buy-sell agreement to produce funds to keep a closely held family business in the family in a situation in which the three brothers running the company were in constant disagreement.

With regard to adequate and full consideration, it is not fair market value. In this case, the value of right to receive moneys upon termination of the split-dollar agreement was adequately supplemented by interest on the long-term loan roughly equaling the inside build-up of the policies, management succession and efficiency, and capital accumulation. The entire agreement protected foreseeable risks to the family business.

The taxpayer in *Estate of Cahill v. Commissioner*[308] was not as fortunate. The Tax Court denied summary judgment that the exception had been met on the grounds that the taxpayer had failed to show that the intent was to provide liquidity decades from now to transfer the family business to the grandchildren, particularly when the loans to produce the funds were only a 5-year term and the internal return of the policies did not cover the interest of the short-term notes. With regard to full and adequate consideration, the decedent's value of the receivable of only $183,700 was clearly not adequate for a $10 million premium transfer.

5. Sections 2703

Section 2703 states that value of property will be set without regard to "any restrictions on the right to sell or use such property."

The IRS argued that when Levine entered into the split-dollar arrangement, she placed a restriction on her right to control the $6.5 million in cash and the life insurance policies. And the restriction on Levine's right to unilaterally access the funds transferred to the insurance companies for the benefit of the ILIT is what should be disregarded when determining the value of the property.

The Tax Court stated that the only property in Levine's estate was her receivable under the split-dollar agreement. There were no restrictions on that property in the agreement. The restrictions referenced by the IRS were on the ILIT and the life insurance policies that were not in Levine's estate. Therefore, Section 2703 does not apply.

Again, the taxpayers in *Cahill* and *Morrissette* were not as fortunate. Because both split-dollar agreements contained a mutual termination provision, the veto power given to the ILIT to prevent termination was a restriction which could be ignored under Section 2703, *Estate of Cahill, Estate of Morrissette* order date February 19, 2019.

However, there is an exception to the exclusion rule under IRC Section 2703(b) if the restriction is a part of a bona fide business arrangement, not a device to transfer property at less than adequate and full consideration and for terms comparable to similar arrangements entered into at arm's length. *Estate of Morrissette v. Commissioner*[309] met the exception (though lost in the valuation of the split-dollar agreement discussed later). The court concluded that there was a bona business purpose to provide liquidity to support the family business and that the mutual termination clause significantly supported that business purpose. The court also concluded that the agreements provided reasonable repayment terms and that the inside build-up of the policies was comparable to the return on long-term bonds. Finally, the court concluded that the acrimonious relationship of the brothers and the disputes over ownership among them would have resulted in an arm's length mutual termination agreement in comparable split-dollar agreements.

6. *Valuation of Discount*

It is very important to retain a qualified appraiser to come up with the value of the split-dollar agreement at the date of death of the grandparent based on the receipt of the greater of premium payments and cash value growth at the death of the insured children perhaps decades in the future. The *Morrissette* case indicated that the annual probability-adjusted expected value of the policy was based on the expected cash surrender value and the probabilities of mortality factors for each year until the anticipated maturity date using a present value discount rate (8.5% and 6.5% in *Morrissette*).

However, to obtain the discount over the life expectancy of the children, there must be no intent at the date of the decedent's death to terminate the split-dollar arrangement at an earlier date. For example, in the *Estate of Morrissette v. Commissioner*,[310] the revocable trust, which became irrevocable at the death of the decedent, stated the trustees had the discretion to distribute the split-dollar agreement receivable to the ILIT, which would have terminated the split-dollar arrangement. Also, there was evidence that some of the brothers wanted to surrender some of the policies shortly after the statute of limitations on the estate's 706 had run. Accordingly, at the request of the IRS, the court determined that the discount would be for only just short of 5 years (rather than the life expectancy of the insured son) because there was evidence that there was a prearranged plan to terminate the split-dollar agreement and some of the insurance policies. The opinion indicated that without the IRS stipulation, it probably would have found an earlier termination date.

Thus, the *Morrissette* taxpayer won the IRC Sections 2036, 2038, and 2703 battles but lost the war because of revocable trust distribution provision to the ILIT and the documented comments of professional advisers and family members that the arrangement would be terminated soon after Mrs. Morrissette's death.

7. *Present Bottom Line for Intergenerational Split-Dollar Economic Benefit Regime*

Based on the *Levine* (and *Cahill* and *Morrissette*) cases, economic benefit regime intergenerational split-dollar should provide as follows:

(1) Have an independent trustee for the ILIT with fiduciary obligations to grandchildren and not just the grandparent and the insured

children. *Levine* would probably have been even stronger if the business associate and power of attorney holder Larson had not been a trustee.

(2) Do not grant the grandparent a right to terminate or modify, either alone or jointly, the split-dollar agreement. (If necessary, give the unilateral right to terminate or modify to the independent trustee of the ILIT.)

(3) The grandparent has a split-dollar receivable equal to the greater of the premium payments or the cash value of the policies.

(4) Make sure that all incidents of ownership are retained by the ILIT in both the ILIT document and any collateral assignment back to the grandparent.

(5) The grandparent should not give or sell the split-dollar receivable to the ILIT during lifetime or at death.

(6) Emails, other documentation, and conversations should not indicate a possible prearranged plan to terminate the split-dollar agreement or to surrender the insurance policies earlier than planned maturity. In other words, the arrangement should be for the long haul after the grandparent's death (unless the situation materially changes after the grandparent's death).

(7) Even if a bona fide sale under IRC Sections 2036(a) and 2038(a)(1) and a bona fide business arrangement under IRC Section 2703(b) are not involved, it is still a good idea to have a significant non-tax reason for the arrangement (e.g., to provide liquidity for business continuity).

8. Does the Loan Regime Avoid These Issues?

As discussed in more detail in Section IV.I. earlier, an intergenerational split-dollar arrangement could be set up under the loan regime with the "donor" receiving a long-term promissory note paying the applicable AFR. If the loan can avoid being classified as equity by qualifying under the Regulation provision by making the required representation, then Sections 2036 and 2038 would not apply. Arguably, there would be no restriction to which

Section 2703 would apply. If the promissory note is for a long term and the donor could not call the note, then the note value would receive a discount, particularly if the discount rate is higher than the AFR. Another advantage of the loan regime is that the payment to the grandparent is limited to the premiums paid (and perhaps accumulated interest), and the equity build-up in the ILIT will be owned by the ILIT.

However, the discount would not be as high as in the economic benefit regime. Also, the AFR might be higher than term premium for the pure death benefit under the economic benefit regime particularly if a second-to-die policy is involved like in *Levine*. The IRS might be able to argue no business purpose. So far, the IRS has not taken an intergenerational loan regime split-dollar arrangement to court. Some practitioners have told the author that the IRS has in the past argued the size of the loan regime discount, and there have been some out of court settlements of up to 65% discount. However, recently, the IRS has been taking a more aggressive stand on fighting against a significant discount in intergenerational loan regime split-dollar promissory notes.

VI. "Grandfathered" Endorsement Split-Dollar Arrangements

A. What Is a "Grandfathered" Endorsement Split-Dollar Arrangement?

The Final Split-Dollar Regulations[311] governing split-dollar arrangements were issued on September 12, 2003, effective on September 18, 2003. The Final Split-Dollar Regulations provide guidance on the issues of what constitute an arrangement "entered into" (which may be applied to determine whether an arrangement was "entered into" before January 28, 2002, for purposes of Notice 2002-8, which doesn't define this term under the Notice) before the effective date of the Regulations and what might (or might not) be a "material modification" to a pre-Final Split-Dollar Regulations arrangement—technically, what would *not* be considered a material modification.

The Regulations apply only to split-dollar life insurance arrangements entered into after September 17, 2003, or "materially modified" thereafter. For these purposes, an arrangement is "entered into" on *the latest of:*

(1) the date the policy subject to the arrangement is issued;

(2) the effective date of the policy subject to the arrangement;

(3) the date the first policy premium is paid;

(4) the date the parties enter into the agreement; and

(5) the date the arrangement satisfies the definition of split-dollar arrangement. The result of this provision will be to postpone the date on which an arrangement can be considered "entered into."

The very short period of time between the announcement and the effective date appears only to have allowed completion of an arrangement that was nearly complete before issuance of the Final Split-Dollar Regulations. In general, the Regulations make it clear that the policy must be issued, paid for, and effective before September 17, 2003, to be treated as a pre-Final Split-Dollar Regulations arrangement, although a signed agreement may not be required by September 17, 2003, if there is evidence that there was a binding contract between the parties under state law. Similarly, the fact that a collateral assignment or an endorsement may not have been filed with the insurer before September 17, 2003, should not prevent an otherwise qualifying arrangement from being treated as pre-September 17, 2003, arrangement.

The Regulations also apply to any arrangement that is "materially modified" after September 17, 2003. The Regulations contain a "non-exclusive" list of non-material modifications; however, given the nature of the items listed, it appears that only minor, ministerial changes will fall within the definition. For example, permitted modifications include a change from monthly to quarterly premiums, a change required to permit the policy to continue to qualify as life insurance or a change in the interest rate for a policy loan. The only "substantive" item on this list is a non-discretionary change made pursuant to a binding commitment between the parties; the Explanation to the Regulations also exempts any change made solely to comply with the safe harbor provisions of Notice 2002-8.

Given the fact that the Preamble to the first set of Proposed Regulations requested comments on whether a Section 1035 exchange of the policy subject to the arrangement should be considered a material modification, its absence from the list of non-material changes and the nature of the other items on that list indicate that a policy exchange should be considered a material modification (regardless of whether the exchange increased the face amount of the policy). In fact, it has been reported that the omission was intentional; Treasury was apparently worried about "creative" policy designs they couldn't anticipate.

The full list of non-material modifications in the Final Split-Dollar Regulations is as follows:

(1) a change solely in the mode of premium payment (e.g., a change from monthly to quarterly premiums);

(2) a change solely in the beneficiary of the life insurance contract, unless the beneficiary is a party to the arrangement;

(3) a change solely in the interest rate payable under the life insurance contract on a policy loan;

(4) a change solely necessary to preserve the status of the life insurance contract under Section 7702;

(5) a change solely to the ministerial provisions of the life insurance contract (e.g., a change in the address to send payment);

(6) a change made solely under the terms of any agreement (other than the life insurance contract) that is a part of the split-dollar life insurance arrangement if the change is non-discretionary by the parties and is made pursuant to a binding commitment (whether set forth in the agreement or otherwise) in effect on or before September 17, 2003;

(7) a change solely in the owner of the life insurance contract as a result of a transaction to which Section 381(a) applies and in which substantially all of the former owner's assets are transferred to the new owner of the policy;

(8) a change to the policy solely if such change is required by a court or a state insurance commissioner as a result of the insolvency of the insurance company that issued the policy; or

(9) a change solely in the insurance company that administers the policy as a result of an assumption reinsurance transaction between the issuing insurance company and the new insurance company to which the owner and the non-owner were not a party.

In addition, the Final Split-Dollar Regulations provide that the Commissioner, in revenue rulings, notices, and other guidance published in the *Internal Revenue Bulletin*, may provide additional guidance with respect to other modifications that are not material.

B. The Prior Law on Split-Dollar Arrangements—Before the Notices and the Final Split-Dollar Regulations

The IRS definition of split-dollar life insurance arrangements was historically set forth in Rev. Rul. 64-328,[312] which was revoked, as obsolete, for post-Final Split-Dollar Regulation arrangements and even for pre-Final Split-Dollar Regulation arrangements except to the extent described in Notice 2002-8 by Rev. Rul. 2003-105.[313] This ruling accompanied the adoption of the Final Split-Dollar Regulations, which have their own broad definition of split-dollar arrangements. Rev. Rul. 64-328 generally defined the arrangement as a sharing of the costs (and benefits) of a life insurance policy between (in that context) an employer and an employee (and his or her beneficiaries)—an employer providing an employee with life insurance protection for his or her family as a part of an employee benefit plan. Again, the definition in the Final Split-Dollar Regulations is much broader and would, for instance, include an interest-bearing loan to a policy owner secured by a policy as well as a private donor–donee economic benefit arrangement.

In employment-related arrangements, economically, the employer is advancing the premiums due on a permanent policy insuring the employee (or someone selected by the employee) for the benefit of the employee's (or the insured's) named beneficiary(ies) or for the policy owner(s); the employer will have its advances returned, without interest, at the insured's death (out of the death proceeds of the policy) or upon earlier termination of the arrangement during the insured's lifetime (out of the policy's cash value).

Despite the possible analysis of these transactions as interest-free loans, for historical reasons, the ruling held that they were not interest-free loans but were instead the employer providing the insured employee with an economic benefit of having his or her life insured—a taxable employment benefit (except to the extent that amount was contributed by the employee); even though the employee is taxable on the benefit, there is no deduction for the employer for the cost of the benefit.[314] Under Rev. Rul. 64-328, the same benefit was held to be provided to the employee, regardless of the form of the transaction—that is, which party owned the policy; for arrangements subject to the Final Split-Dollar Regulations, policy ownership (or deemed ownership) generally will for the first time determine whether the arrangement will be treated as an interest-free loan or an economic benefit transaction.

Under Rev. Rul. 64-328, the measure of that economic benefit was the term insurance cost of providing that net or pure death benefit, determined under a table known as the PS 58 rates or (electively) under Rev. Rul. 66-110, similarly revoked by Rev. Rul. 2003-105, the insurer's lower, generally available published 1-year term rate. The issue of whether a particular alternative term rate qualifies under Rev. Rul. 66-110 has been the subject of a number of unfavorable letter rulings.[315] Finally, under Notice 2002-8,[316] Table 2001 continues to be available; for arrangements entered into after January 28, 2002, however, alternative term rates will have to meet similar (but more stringent) additional tests after 2003 (but pre-January 28,

2002, arrangements will be exempt from those additional requirements). Table 2001 is attached as Appendix 1; a comparison of the PS 58 rates, the Table 2001 rates, and one carrier's alternative term rates at given ages is attached as Appendix 2.

Rev. Rul. 66-110 also provided that any "other benefit" other than current insurance protection (an undefined phrase) provided to the insured under the plan was taxable (which arguably could apply to policy cash values that exceed cumulative employer premiums, when the employer is limited to recovering only its premiums, so-called policy "equity"). Notices 2001-10 and 2002-8 chose not to apply this "other benefit" analysis to the taxation of policy equity; instead, they applied the Section 83 transfer of property theory of Technical Advice Memorandum (TAM) 9604001. However, the Proposed and Final Split-Dollar Regulations adopt something like the Rev. Rul. 66-110 "other benefit" theory (under Section 61) to tax policy equity currently based on access for endorsement arrangements subject to the Regulations.

Until the issuance of the Notices and the adoption of the Final Split-Dollar Regulations, most of what was known about the income tax consequences of employment-related, corporate-shareholder, or private (donor–donee) split-dollar life insurance arrangements was derived from Rev. Rul. 64-328 (and to a lesser extent, Rev. Rul. 66-110); they were both issued in an employment context and had been central in understanding the tax consequences of the split-dollar concept. This has historically been true not only for income tax purposes but for transfer tax purposes (i.e., gift, estate, and generation-skipping transfer tax) as well. The rulings that extended these income tax conclusions to the transfer tax context are Rev. Ruls. 78-420[317] (also revoked as obsolete for post-Final Split-Dollar Regulation arrangements by Rev. Rul. 2003-105) and 81-198[318] (which wasn't revoked as obsolete for those purposes), both of which held that in a third party–owned arrangement, the measure of the employee's income was also the measure of his or her gift to the policy owner; they provide the transfer tax leverage for split-dollar but also seem to require that policy equity be treated as a gift (if it is subject to income tax on a current basis).

However, going forward, Notice 2002-8 (for pre-Final Regulation arrangements) and the Final Split-Dollar Regulations for (post-Final Regulation arrangements) will be the only sources of authority on split-dollar arrangements for both income and transfer tax purposes. In fact, as noted, Rev. Rul. 2003-105, which accompanied the publication of the Final Split-Dollar

Regulations, revoked the prior rulings as obsolete for post-Final Split-Dollar Regulation arrangements (and for pre-Final Split-Dollar Regulation arrangements except to the extent their principles were incorporated into Notice 2002-8).

In general, the concept of split-dollar arrangements is derived from Rev. Rul. 64-328 and a series of later public and private letter rulings; there is no statutory nor (until the Final Split-Dollar Regulations were adopted) was there any regulatory underpinning for the concept.

Because under the theory of Rev. Rul. 64-328, the measure of the income tax consequences of the arrangement and, under the other rulings discussed earlier, of any gift resulting from the arrangement where a third party (e.g., a trust) owns the employee's interest in the policy, were traditionally the so-called "economic benefit" to the employee—not the employer's premium advances. That is what creates "leverage" in the arrangement for both income and gift tax (and when the gift benefits "skip persons," potentially for GST tax) purposes. That is, the income (and transfer) tax consequences of a split-dollar arrangement to the insured employee are reduced from the amount of the policy premium advanced by the premium provider for the permanent insurance protection provided to essentially the cost of an equivalent amount of pure term insurance. That leverage is especially pronounced when joint life policies are used in these arrangements because of the reduced "economic benefit" of such policies, at least while both insureds are alive, as Notice 2002-8 confirms.

C. Notice 2002-8[319]

Notice 2002-8, which was issued on January 3, 2002, revokes Notice 2001-10 (the prior Notice governing pre-Final Split-Dollar Regulation arrangements). However, Table 2001 was republished in this Notice, and the revocation of Rev. Rul. 55-747[320] and modification of Rev. Ruls. 64-328[321] and 66-110[322] announced in Notice 2001-10 remain effective. Finally, taxpayers may, if they wish, rely on either Notice 2001-10 or Notice 2002-8 for the income and gift tax treatment of pre-Final Split-Dollar Regulations arrangements.

The Notice announces the Service's intent to publish Proposed Regulations and provides an outline of the provisions expected to be included in the Proposed Regulations; the Proposed and the Final Split-Dollar Regulations themselves are, however, substantially different than the expected Proposed

Regulations described in the Notice. Because the description of the expected Proposed Regulations in Notice 2002-8 differs in so many respects from the Proposed and the Final Split-Dollar Regulations themselves, that portion of the Notice won't be described here.

The Notice also provides guidance on the value of the "economic benefit" generated by split-dollar arrangements and additional "interim" rules for the taxation of arrangements entered into before the final guidance.

1. Revised Standards for Valuing Current Life Insurance Protection

The Notice provides updated interim guidance on the value of current life insurance protection under a split-dollar arrangement.

Parties to pre-January 28, 2002, arrangements may continue to use "the insurer's lower published premium rates that are available to all standard risks for initial issue one-year term insurance" to measure the value of the current life insurance protection provided under a split-dollar arrangement, assuming these rates meet the requirements set out in Rev. Ruls. 66-110 and 67-154. These rates will not be required to meet the additional criteria, discussed later, for post–January 28, 2002, arrangements. This is much more generous than Notice 2001-10, which imposed the stricter requirements for the use of alternative term rates on all arrangements beginning after December 31, 2003. However, as a practical matter, if the insurer creates new rates to meet the 2003 requirements, it may not be able to maintain a separate set of published term rates for these grandfathered policies.

Parties to a pre–January 28, 2002, arrangement will also have the option of using the Table 2001 rates (republished as a part of this Notice) to measure the value of the current life insurance protection under a split-dollar arrangement and can use these rates to determine rates for survivorship policies (as described later).

For post–January 28, 2002, or pre-future guidance arrangements, the use of the P.S. 58 rates is not available, but parties to these arrangements may use the Table 2001 rates to measure current life insurance protection.

The Notice further provides, "Taxpayers should make appropriate adjustments to these premium rates if the life insurance protection covers more than one life." This appears to provide authority for what many have believed to be the case under Notice 2001-10; specifically, that with the revocation of Rev. Rul. 55-747,[323] survivorship term rates should be determined by inserting the Table 2001 rates into the formula described in the so-called "Greenberg to Greenberg" letter. A joint and survivor Table 2001 is attached as Appendix 3.

Parties to these arrangements will also be able to use the insurer's lower alternative term rates, which satisfy the requirements of Rev. Ruls. 66-110[324] and 67-154[325] to measure the current life insurance protection under a split-dollar arrangement. However, after December 31, 2003, the insurer's rates will be deemed not to meet those requirements unless:

> (i) [t]he insurer generally makes the availability of such rates known to persons who apply for term insurance coverage from the insurer, and (ii) the insurer regularly sells term insurance at such rates to individuals who apply for term insurance coverage through the insurer's normal distribution channels.

Thus, alternative term rates will remain available, although they are likely to be higher as they are adjusted to meet these new standards, and many carriers no longer publish term rates that meet these standards. In fact, many carriers will no longer provide a determination that their rates meet these standards, on the theory that it is a legal question; instead, they will provide information about how many term policies were sold at these rates and let this insured's advisors determine whether it had "regularly" sold policies at these rates.

2. *Interim Guidance for the Tax Treatment of Pre-Final Split-Dollar Regulations Arrangements*

a. Economic Benefit Treatment

Under the Notice, for split-dollar arrangements entered into before the date of publication of Final Split-Dollar Regulations, there will be no deemed transfer of any policy equity under Section 83 *solely* because the cash value of a policy exceeds the amount due the "service recipient" under the arrangement; presumably, a termination of the arrangement would be treated as a transfer of the entire policy, and a withdrawal by the employee of any portion of the policy equity would be treated as a transfer of that amount. "Service recipient" is the term used in the Notice and is distinguishable from the more generic term "sponsor" used in most of the other provisions of this section of the Notice. It is likely this distinction simply reflects the fact that Section 83 would not apply, for example, to a private split-dollar arrangement. In addition, the provisions discussed next appear to provide similar protection to the more generic "benefited person" under a non–service-related split-dollar arrangement.

Similarly, if parties to a pre-Final Split-Dollar Regulations arrangement treat the value of the current life insurance protection as a benefit provided "by a sponsor to a benefited person" (presumably applying the provision to non–service-related arrangements), "the Service will not treat the arrangement as having been terminated" and, accordingly, will not treat the arrangement as involving a transfer of any policy equity to the benefited person, "so long as the parties to the arrangement continue to treat and report the value of the life insurance protection as an economic benefit provided to the benefited person." This rule will apply as long as the sponsor has *any* economic interest in the policy, no matter how small (although it seems prudent not to reduce that interest to a nominal amount). This would allow the premium provider to recover most (but not all) of its advances, without triggering tax on policy equity (caused by a termination of the arrangement). This may lead to the odd result that if a sponsor is partially repaid—assuming death benefit remains constant—the economic benefit cost would increase because it is measured based on the benefited person's share of the death benefit.

Although not stated explicitly, it seems implicit (by negative inference) that if such an arrangement is terminated (other than as a result of the insured's death), there would be a deemed termination of the arrangement and a deemed transfer of the policy equity. This deemed transfer would then presumably be taxed under Section 83 if in the employment context, as a gift; in a private split-dollar arrangement; or, generally, in accordance with the rules that would apply given the relationship of the parties.

b. Loan Treatment

Parties to a pre-Final Split-Dollar Regulations arrangement may also elect to treat it as a loan, and if this election is made, "the Service will not challenge reasonable efforts to comply with the requirements of Sections 1271–1275 and Section 7872." If such an arrangement is treated as a loan, all payments made before the date the decision is made to treat it as a loan must be treated as a loan made as of the first day of the year in which the election is made. It appears that as long as the arrangement meets the "pre-date of Final Split-Dollar Regulations" requirement, the parties may elect loan treatment at any time during the course of the arrangement, although a post-January 28, 2002, arrangement would have no equity grandfathering for such a conversion, which would be treated as a termination of the arrangement, with resultant transfer of any policy equity.

Under Section 7872, the parties can arrange to tax the interest element over the term of the loan—all at once at the outset of the arrangement (as OID) by providing it is a term loan or each year by providing that the loan is a demand loan. Most employment-related arrangements would likely be demand loans in any event because they would be terminable on termination of employment. In a term loan, the rate is fixed at the outset, but in a demand loan, it varies each year. If the parties want to lock in a rate over the term of a loan at the outset but does not have the unstated interest treated as OID, they would have to document the arrangement as an interest-bearing term loan, with AFR interest payable annually, or accrued and paid with the principal.

Treating a split-dollar arrangement as an interest-free loan for tax purposes would solve any possible equity issues for split-dollar arrangements because any increases in value of property purchased with a loan (interest free or otherwise) shouldn't be treated as provided by the premium provider and therefore taxable (until otherwise realized—here by cashing in or surrendering the policy); this result was confirmed by the Notice. In addition, treating the arrangement as an interest-free loan might in fact be economically preferable for older insureds (at least in the later years of the arrangement) because, for them, the measure of taxation under Section 7872 could be lower than under the economic benefit concept (which is term insurance cost driven).

However, applying Section 7872 to a split-dollar arrangement would mean that the calculation of the Section 7872 measure of taxation would become more complex (based on the characterization of the loan and the appropriate AFR), and unlike the economic benefit concept, could in some circumstances generate income to the employer in an employment context. In addition, the timing of the income generated by the arrangement would change depending on whether the "loan" were considered a term loan (in which case all of the income over the expected term—based on life expectancy—would be lumped in the arrangement's initial year, as OID) or a demand loan (in which case the income would be reported each year). Finally, for third-party transactions, the "double loan" consequences of an interest-free loan—treating the transaction as a loan to the employee and then a reloan from the employee to the owner—would introduce income tax consequences to the third-party owner unless it were a grantor trust (and would complicate the transfer tax implications of these split-dollar arrangements). For loans that provide for AFR interest, the loan is treated made directly by the lender to the third-party owner, eliminating the insured as an indirect party to the loan.

In an employment setting, if the premium advances made in a split-dollar life insurance arrangement were treated under Section 7872 as below market loans to the insured, the amount of foregone interest on such payments would be treated as having been first transferred from the employer to the employee and then retransferred by the employee back to the employer as interest under Section 7872(a)(1) for income tax purposes; this would create compensation income for the employee (and a corresponding compensation deduction for the employer) and interest income for the employer (and a likely non-deductible interest expense for the employee). This results only if the aggregate outstanding amount of the loans from the employer to the employee, made for purposes other than for tax avoidance, including such premium advances exceeds $10,000 under the de minimis rule of Section 7872(c)(3).

Under Section 7872(e)(2), the term "foregone interest" means, with respect to any period when the loan is outstanding, the excess of the amount of interest which would have been payable on the loan for the period if interest, payable annually, had accrued on the loan at the AFR, over any interest payable on the loan properly allocable to such period.

For private split-dollar arrangements treated as below-market loans subject to Section 7872, the premium provider (lender) would be treated as having transferred the interest to the policy owner (borrower) for gift and GST purposes and to have received interest income from the owner (unless the owner were a grantor trust from the point of view of the lender, in which case the interest would be ignored for income tax purposes).

As noted earlier, the amounts deemed transferred (and when such amounts must be recognized for tax purposes by the employer and employee) will depend on when the premium advances are to be repaid. If the premiums are to be repaid at an ascertainable date in the future (including one that is actuarially determinable, such as[326] upon the death of the insured), the advances will be treated as term loans. If the premiums are to be repaid at any time on the demand of the employer or if the employee's interest in the arrangement is not transferable and is conditioned on the future performance of substantial services by the employee (within the meaning of Section 83), the advances will be treated as demand loans.[327]

As noted earlier, the date on which the transfer and retransfer of the foregone interest between the parties will be deemed to have occurred will depend on whether the premium advances are treated as term loans or demand loans. For demand loans, the foregone interest attributable to periods during any calendar year is generally treated as transferred and retransferred on December 31st of that calendar year.[328] In the case of term loans, the amount of the deemed transfer is treated as transferred at the time the loan is made and is equal to the excess of the amount loaned over the present value of all payments that are required to be made under the terms of the loan agreement, bunching all of the foregone interest into the first year of the arrangement.[329]

The retransfer as interest under term loans is deemed to occur over the period the amount of the loan is unpaid; for demand loans, the foregone interest attributable to any calendar year is generally treated as retransferred on December 31st of that calendar year under Section 7872(a)(2). Accordingly, if the below-market compensatory loan is a term loan, the inclusion and deductions resulting from the arrangement will be mismatched—income will be bunched in the first year, and any deductions will be spread out over the life of the loan.

With a third-party owner in an employment-related arrangement, as discussed in more detail earlier, the interest would be deemed to have been loaned to the employee by the employer and reloaned by the employee to the owner for both income and gift tax purposes, resulting in a gift to the trust and generating interest income to the employee.[330] However, if the trust were a grantor trust for income tax purposes (as most insurance trusts are), there would be no income tax consequences from the reloan because transactions between grantors and their grantor trusts are ignored for income tax purposes under Rev. Rul. 85-13.[331]

Instead of attempting to comply with the interest-free loan rules of Section 7872, consideration could be given to structuring (or restructuring) any such arrangement as an *interest-bearing loan transaction* using the AFR, presumably on a term loan basis, and documenting it as a loan (or premium financing) transaction rather than as economic benefit split-dollar arrangement. This would allow the parties to "lock in" the interest rate applicable to each loan for the long term (if it were financially advantageous to do so, as in the current low interest rate environment).

Note also that in an employment context, this concept could raise state law issues relating to the employer's ability to make loans to executives who were shareholders or directors; could violate bank or other restrictions applicable to the employer; and if the policies acquired with the proceeds of the loan were variable policies (which presumably would be "margin stock"), could require application of the margin rules of Regulation U of the Federal Reserve Board. However, although unless the employer were otherwise subject to these rules—for instance, a bank—unless it originated more than $200,000 or more in margin stock loans in a calendar quarter or had $500,000 or more of such loans outstanding in a calendar quarter, these rules wouldn't apply.

c. Effect on Other Documents

As noted earlier, Notice 2001-10[332] was revoked. However, as also noted earlier, Table 2001 was republished and the changes made by Notice 2001-10 to Rev. Ruls. 55-747,[333] 64-328,[334] and 66-110[335] remain in effect; taxpayers may continue to rely on Notice 2001-10 if they wish.

d. "No Inference"

Importantly, Section VI of Notice 2002-8 contains the following so-called "no inference" language:

> [N]o inference should be drawn from this notice regarding the appropriate federal income, employment and gift tax treatment of split-dollar life insurance arrangements entered into before the date of publication of final regulations. However, taxpayers may rely on this notice (including a reasonable application of the rules to be proposed as described in Part II) or Notice 2001-10 for split-dollar life insurance arrangements entered into before the date of publication of final regulations.

The intent and scope of this ambiguous provision are unclear; it was apparently an attempt by the Service to react to the insurance industry's desire for "grandfathering" for pre-existing equity arrangements; it is clearly not the grandfathering industry hoped for. It seems incongruous to allow practitioners to rely on the Notice but to provide no inference can be drawn from the Notice. Does this provision mean the Service cannot rely on the Notice to tax pre-Final Regulation arrangements? In any event, practitioners have used it to argue that policy equity, in such arrangements, will not be taxable to the benefited party either as it accrues nor even when the split-dollar arrangement terminates before the insured's death based on the absence of pre-Notice law holding it taxable in either instance.

With respect to this issue, this provision has been interpreted to mean that for all split-dollar arrangements entered into before and not materially modified after September 17, 2003 (the effective date of the Final Split-Dollar Regulations), the Service may not use this Notice (or Notice 2001-10 or the Proposed or Final Split-Dollar Regulations) as support for the position that policy equity is taxable (although it would presumably taken that position on audit based on pre-Notice, pre-Regulation law). Similarly, a taxpayer would not be able to invoke either the Notice or the Regulations to argue that any of them represented a change in the law and that therefore the equity would not have been taxable under prior law. Essentially, both the Service and the taxpayer would be required to rely on the law as it existed before Notice 2001-10 for purposes of making or defending a claim that policy equity in an equity split-dollar arrangement should be taxed on termination of the arrangement.

Furthermore, under the interim guidance provisions of the 2002 Notice, Section IV, paragraph 1 states:

> For split-dollar life insurance arrangements entered into before the date of publication of final regulations, the Service will not treat a service recipient as having made a transfer of a portion of the cash surrender value of a life insurance contract to a service provider for purposes of section 83 solely because the interest or other earnings credited to the cash surrender value of the contract cause the cash surrender value to exceed the portion thereof payable to the service recipient.

Therefore, although traditionally, there was uncertainty not only about whether policy equity would be taxed but also, if it was taxable, when taxation would occur, the 2002 Notice provides that the Service will not attempt to tax policy equity unless and until the arrangement terminates before the insured's death.

e. When Are "Arrangements Entered Into"?

A number of the provisions of the Notice are applicable to "arrangements entered into" before a particular date or event. That raises issues both as to what is required to enter into an arrangement and whether any change to the arrangement (or even to the policy subject to the arrangement) could affect the ability to hold the date of the arrangement—whether there is any risk or modification of the arrangement after a critical date would create a new arrangement under the Notice.

It seems that an agreement alone, without a policy issued or at least applied for, would not sufficiently bind the parties to create a pre-relevant date arrangement. On the other hand, if it is not possible to have the policy issued or applied for by the relevant date, there seems to be no downside to creating the arrangement before the relevant date so that the parties might at least have an argument for the pre-relevant date status of the arrangement (although if they would not enter into the arrangement without pre-relevant date protection, they should be advised of this risk of such an arrangement). Note that the Final Split-Dollar Regulations provide a detailed definition of arrangements entered into before their adoption, which might be applied by the Service under the Notice.

Although the Notice is silent on this point, a substantial modification (however that is ultimately defined) of an arrangement entered into before a relevant date could possibly eliminate the status of the arrangement as "pre-relevant date" (assuming the modification was made after the relevant date). For example, the Final Split-Dollar Regulations apply to a pre-Final Split-Dollar Regulations arrangement that is "materially modified" after issuance of the Regulations. But note again that the Notice does not, by its terms, contain such a concept (possibly indicating that no such concept will apply for purposes of the Notice).

It is unclear whether an exchange or modification of a policy after the relevant date would affect the status of the arrangement to which the policy was subject as a pre-relevant date arrangement because it appears to be "arrangements," not policies, on which the dates are keyed. However, a substantial increase in face amount could well be viewed as a substantial modification of the arrangement, as has been the case in prior changes to the split-dollar rules; see, for example, the grandfathering of policies from the changes to the controlling shareholder rules made by Rev. Rul. 82-145.[336] Note, however, that although the Proposed Regulations asked for comments on this issue, the Final Split-Dollar Regulations contain a "non-exclusive" list of non-material modifications that doesn't include policy exchanges.

3. *Summary of Options*

In general, the options available for the parties to a pre–January 28, 2002, arrangement are to continue traditional split-dollar treatment for life (under the implicit safe harbor), with ever-increasing economic benefit costs or to continue traditional split-dollar treatment and then roll out or convert the arrangement to loan treatment in the future (risking taxation of any equity that exists at that point for income and/or transfer tax purposes), relying on the "no inference" language of the Notice for not reporting the equity as taxable—what has been called "wait-and-see (until someone else's client gets audited) split-dollar arrangement."

VII. The Impact of Section 409A on Premium Financing and Economic Benefit Split-Dollar Arrangements

Because of the Enron and WorldCom scandals, Congress imposed significant additional restrictions on the taxation of nonqualified deferred compensation and imposed penalties on taxpayers who failed to comply with new Section 409A. The new statute was effective January 1, 2005. There are restrictions on distribution events, prohibition of benefit acceleration, and restrictions on deferral and redeferral elections.[337] The new law established new taxable funding rules for purposes of Section 83 with regard to offshore property in a rabbi trust, employer financial health triggers for payment, and trusts established or funded during a restricted period when the employer's defined benefit plan is at risk.[338] Finally, if the plan fails to meet or operate in accordance with these requirements, unless the compensation is subject to a substantial risk of forfeiture, the deferred income is immediately taxed, an additional 20% tax is imposed, and interest equal to underpayment rate plus 1% is charged for period of deferral until date of violation of the statutory requirements.[339]

Several preliminary items should be understood about the relationship of Section 409A to premium financing and economic benefit split-dollar arrangements.

(1) Only compensatory arrangements involving employees or other service providers can be covered. Thus arrangements involving donor–donee or corporation–shareholder do not have to comply with Section 409A.

(2) Compensatory arrangements with pre-2005 deferrals are grandfathered to the extent the employee–service provider had a legally binding right to be paid and the right is earned and vested as of December 31, 2004.[340]

(3) With regard to arrangements entered into on or after January 1, 2005, as discussed later, only a very few would not be exempt from Section 409A.

The final Section 409A regulations are silent about premium financing and split-dollar arrangements. However, the Preamble to the proposed regulation does discuss the relationship between Section 409A and these arrangements.[341] At the same time the final Section 409A regulations were issued, the IRS issued Notice 2007-34[342] giving "guidance regarding the application of Section 409A to split-dollar life insurance arrangements."

A. Section 409A and Non-Grandfathered Economic Benefit Split-Dollar Arrangements

(1) If the economic benefit split-dollar arrangement is subject to the Final Split-Dollar Regulations and is not grandfathered from the Regulations and only provides the non-owner service provider a pure death benefit, then it is excluded from Section 409A as a death benefit plan.[343] Also, the compensation described as cost of current life insurance protection on the pure death benefit is also treated as provided under a death benefit plan.[344]

(2) If, under the terms of the arrangement and the relevant facts and circumstances, the non-owner service provider has a legally binding right during a taxable year to any other economic benefit that, pursuant to the terms of the arrangement is payable in a later year, such benefit could be deferred compensation under Section 409A unless it qualifies as a short-term deferral.[345] Examples include current access to policy cash value or other economic benefits under the Final Split-Dollar Regulations.[346] The most common service provider current access to policy cash value is when the service provider owns the cash value in excess of the employer's premium payments, so-called equity split-dollar arrangements.[347] Because normally, such current access by the non-owner results in immediate taxation of the equity under the Final Split-Dollar Regulations,[348] equity split-dollar arrangements are rare.

But even if there is equity in the policy accessible to the non-owner, there would be no deferral subject to Section 409A because, as indicated earlier, it would normally be immediately taxable. However, there is a very narrow area in which a deferral subject to Section 409A could apply—the employee cannot currently borrow or withdraw the equity, but the employer or the employer's general creditors can access the equity. "Current access" to vested equity that is immediately taxable is defined as "currently is directly or indirectly accessible by the non-owner, inaccessible to the owner, or inaccessible to the owner's general creditors."[349] Thus, if the employee is denied access to the equity but the employer and the employer's general creditors have access to it, the arrangement fails the definition, and the equity is not immediately taxable to the employee. Thus, if the equity is vested in the employee and payable in a future taxable year and the Final Split-Dollar Regulations do not make it immediately taxable, Section 409A could apply, resulting in immediate taxation and a 20% penalty tax.

Even ignoring the tax consequences, a key executive is not going to like an arrangement in which the executive's equity can be reached by the employer and the employer's creditors. It would be a better result to have the executive able to currently access the equity and pay an immediate tax under Section 61 rather than an immediate tax plus a 20% penalty tax under Section 409A. It is easy to see why equity split-dollar arrangements are rare after September 17, 2003.

(3) If the employer promises in the split-dollar arrangement to pay the policy premiums in future years, does Section 409A apply? The Preamble to the final Section 409A regulations states that "the arrangement may provide for a deferral of compensation within the meaning of Section 409A" when the employer "irrevocably promises to pay premiums in future years."[350] The key word in the Preamble is "irrevocably." If the employer irrevocably promises in one taxable year to pay premium for the duration of the split-dollar contract that covers premiums in future years, it meets the definition of deferred compensation, and to avoid the Section 409A tax rules, the split-dollar arrangement must have the required Section 409A provisions, which limits the flexibility of the split-dollar arrangement. This problem is easily avoided by making the premium payments contingent on the insured employee continuing to be employed by the employer. This would constitute a substantial risk of forfeiture and the Section 409A deferrals begin at vesting. Because the economic benefit of the premium payment will occur on the date of vesting at the lapse of the substantial risk of forfeiture, there would be no deferral. Most compensatory economic benefit split-dollar arrangements are drafted with the premium payments subject to a substantial risk of forfeiture.

B. Section 409A and Non-Grandfathered Premium Financing Arrangements (Loan Regime)

Likewise, premium financing loans, if not grandfathered from the 409A regulation, normally are not subject to Section 409A.[351] This is logical because a loan involves a creditor and a debtor and is not a compensatory relationship between an employee–service provider and an employer–service recipient. In other words, there is no compensation to be deferred.

However, there are two possible situations of deferral of compensation for loan regime arrangements under Section 409A, one referenced in Notice 2007-34 and the other in the Preamble to the proposed Section 409A regulations.

(1) The Notice states: "In certain situations, such an arrangement may give rise to deferrals of compensation for purposes of Section 409A, for example, if amounts on a split-dollar loan are waived, cancelled, or forgiven."[352] It is difficult to come up with a waiver situation that would result in deferral of compensation under Section 409A—waivers result in immediate income taxation.

A waiver, cancellation, or forgiveness of a loan could result in immediate taxation to the debtor employee–service provider, but it would be difficult to structure a situation in which a deferral under Section 409A would be involved. If the employer at the date the loan was executed never intended to enforce payment, then there would not be any loan but outright immediate taxable compensation.[353] Likewise, if the loan is valid and enforceable at the beginning but the employer decides to cancel it during its term, again the cancelled loan will be subject to immediate taxation at the date of cancellation with no deferral.[354]

What if a "forgivable loan" is involved? This is a loan that provides that it will be extinguished without payment if the employee continues service for the employer for a specified period of time. The argument is that if the arrangement is structured as a bona fide loan and the parties treat it as such, the income is realized at the date of waiver and not at the beginning of the loan. However, the IRS looks closely at forgivable loans to make sure they are not an advance disguised as a loan.[355] If the loan is ignored, there would be immediate taxation of the "loan" as an advance. If the loan is legitimate, then it is a loan and not a deferral until the waiver. Even if the loan is treated as a deferral of compensation, it is subject to a substantial risk of forfeiture.[356] Because the waiver of indebtedness and immediate income taxation occurs upon the expiration of the risk of forfeiture, the short-term exception to the definition of deferred compensation would be applicable even if Section 409A applies because deferral is measured from the date of vesting at the termination of the risk of forfeiture.[357]

(2) The Preamble to the proposed Section 409A regulations, in addition to citing deferral of compensation with regard to loan forgiveness, also states that a deferral of compensation might be involved if there is "no obligation on the part of the service recipient to continue to make premium payments without charging the service provider a market interest rate."[358] Note that this provision was not carried over to Notice 2007-34. Perhaps the IRS has dropped it, or perhaps it is still alive as a "certain situation" under the Notice.[359]

But if the "marketable interest rate" requirement is still in existence, there are a lot of unanswered questions about its application. What is marketable interest rate? Is it the AFR or the current commercial rate that is likely to be higher than the AFR? There is no definition in the Preamble. Furthermore, like the waiver, cancellation, and forgiveness exception, it is difficult to conjure up a situation in which the failure to charge the marketable interest rate results in deferred compensation. To the extent that the AFR rules apply to a below market loan, the employee would be immediately taxed on income for the difference between the AFR and the interest actually paid (no deferral in this case). If the marketable interest rate exceeds the AFR, does the Preamble suggest that the excess over AFR is deferred compensation? It seems inconsistent to have Section 7872 apply current income only up to the AFR but to have Section 409A treat the marketable interest rate in excess of AFR as deferred compensation. Hopefully, the failure to carry over the marketable interest rate exception from the Preamble to the Notice means that this is not an issue to the IRS.

C. The Murky Rules Concerning Section 409A Grandfathered Split-Dollar Arrangements

Section 409A applies to (1) amounts deferred in taxable years beginning after December 31, 2004, and (2) amounts deferred in taxable years beginning before January 1, 2005, if the plan under which the deferral was made is materially modified after October 3, 2004.[360] A modification of a plan is a material modification if a benefit or right is added, and such material enhancement or addition affects amounts earned and vested before 2005. Such material benefit enhancement or addition is a material modification whether it occurs pursuant to an amendment or to the service recipient's exercise of discretion under the terms of the plan.[361] Section 409A does not apply to amounts deferred before January 1, 2005 (or earnings on such deferrals after 2004), if (1) the service provider before January 1, 2005, had a legally binding right to be paid the amount and (2) the right was earned and vested.[362]

There are several rules to be taken from this definition. First, a deferred compensation plan may be partially grandfathered—vested deferrals before 2005 and vested deferrals after 2004 are in the same plan. Second, if there were deferrals before 2005 but they were subject to a substantial risk of forfeiture on December 31, 2004, the entire plan is subject to Section 409A, and none is grandfathered because it was not an earned and vested right on the last day of 2004. Third, the earnings received by the plan after 2004 that are allocable to the grandfathered portion of the plan are themselves grandfathered unless they are subject to a separate substantial risk of forfeiture.[363]

So how do these rules apply to split-dollar arrangements? For premium financing through loans, whether grandfathered or not, there should be no deferral because the cash value is accessible as a creditor by the employer up to the amount of the loan, and the employee currently owns any cash value in excess of the loan unless something comes from the waiver and marketable interest discussions cited previously. For endorsement economic benefit split-dollar arrangements, whether grandfathered or not, there can be no Section 409A application if the employer owns all of the cash value. This is almost universally the case for split-dollar economic benefit arrangements entered into on or after the Final Split-Dollar Regulations, but many of the split-dollar arrangements entered into before September 18, 2003, may have an equity cash value element attributable to the employee, which may or may not be grandfathered from the Section 409A regulations.[364] Many of the answers are supplied by Notice 2007-34.[365] Thus, equity economic benefit split-dollar arrangements, most of which predate the Final Split-Dollar Regulations, are the ones that might have a deferral of income unless grandfathered from the 409A regulation.

(1) If the split-dollar arrangement has a deferral of compensation and is subject to a substantial risk of forfeiture on December 31, 2004, then the entire economic benefit split-dollar or premium financing arrangement is subject to Section 409A and has to be amended to include the provisions required by the Code and the final 409A regulation.

(2) If the policy is totally earned and vested as of December 31, 2004, and no further premiums are paid nor loans made after 2004, the policy will remain totally grandfathered even though the cash value continues to grow because the cash value earnings (if they also are also earned and vested) are solely attributable to the grandfathered cash value.

(3) If the split-dollar arrangement has deferred compensation that was earned and vested on December 31, 2004, but there are premium payments or additional loans after 2004 that were not themselves earned and vested, then the arrangement is partially grandfathered and partially non-grandfathered, the non-grandfather portion being required to meet the requirements of Section 409A and the final Section 409A regulations.[366] When a split-dollar arrangement containing deferred compensation is partially grandfathered and partially non-grandfathered, the grandfathered component may be calculated under any reasonable method that allocates increases in policy cash value between the grandfathered and non-grandfathered components. A method is not reasonable if it allocates a disproportionate amount of policy costs and expenses to the non-grandfathered component.

There is a safe harbor reasonable proportional allocation by calculating the grandfathered component value by the greater of (1) the cash value that was earned and vested on December 31, 2004 (reduced by any amount securing the amount owed to the employer), and (2) an amount equal to the policy cash value on the valuation date multiplied by a fraction, the numerator of which is the sum of the grandfathered premiums actually paid on the policy and the denominator of which is the sum of all premiums actually paid on the policy by the valuation date.[367]

The Notice defines "grandfathered premiums" as the premiums paid before 2005 and premiums paid after 2004 pursuant to a legally binding right that was itself earned and vested as of December 31, 2004. Thus, premiums paid after 2004, pursuant to a legally binding contractual right that was vested and not subject to a substantial risk of forfeiture on December 31, 2004, will increase the grandfathered component of the policy cash value. However, if the premiums paid after 2004 were not contractually obligated to be paid and would be forfeited if the employee terminated employment (which is the typical endorsement split-dollar arrangement), these premiums will increase the non-grandfathered component of the policy cash value.

(4) The area of the least clarity is the treatment of equity split-dollar arrangements that are not totally grandfathered from the final Section 409A regulations but that are grandfathered from the Final Split-Dollar Regulations. As indicated, the most common split-dollar arrangement before 2003 was an equity split-dollar arrangement that was not a loan, and the employee owned the cash value in excess of the employer's premium payments. Under the Final Split-Dollar Regulations, such direct access to the equity in an endorsement split-dollar arrangement would result in immediate taxation to the employee. However, equity arrangements predating the Final Split-Dollar Regulations are grandfathered from the Regulations, and presumably, prior law would apply. The prior law is unclear as to the taxation of grandfathered equity split-dollar arrangements.[368] If it is taxable, then it would be taxable under Section 83 as a transfer of property in return for services rendered.

Does Section 409A apply to these equity split-dollar arrangements that are grandfathered from the Final Split-Dollar Regulations but not from the Section 409A regulation (e.g., the employee's interest was subject to a substantial risk of forfeiture on December 31, 2004)? It is not clear. Notice 2007-34 does state that Section 409A does not apply to a pre-September 18, 2003 equity split-dollar agreement as long as "the parties to the arrangement continue to treat and report the value of the life insurance protection as an economic benefit provided to the benefited person" and meet all other requirements of Notice 2002-8.[369] This appears to say that the IRS will not apply Section 409A to equity endorsement split-dollar grandfathered arrangements as long as either the employee is paying the term premium for the employee's cost of current life insurance protection or the employer includes such premium on the employee's W-2. The problem is that the term premium may get so high as the employee grows older that the split-dollar arrangement has to be terminated before the insured's death to avoid an insupportable economic benefit.

What happens if the safe harbor provision of Notice 2002-8 and Notice 2007-34 ends when the equity endorsement split-dollar arrangement is terminated during the lifetime of the insured? There isn't a definitive answer.

Notice 2002-8 states that "no inference should be drawn from this Notice regarding the appropriate Federal income, employment and gift tax treatment of split-dollar insurance arrangements entered into before the date of publication of Final Split-Dollar Regulations."[370] Some practitioners took this to mean that the IRS was not going after the grandfathered equity split-dollar arrangement and would just concentrate on arrangements covered by the Final Split-Dollar Regulations. But the quoted language seems to state that it is giving no guidance in this area rather than exempting split-dollar regulation equity split-dollar from taxation. However, to date, the author knows of no situation when the IRS has attacked grandfathered equity split-dollar arrangements.[371] Note that Notice 2007-34, although it references other provisions of Notice 2002-8, doesn't contain "no inference" language.

Notice 2007-34 raises the possibility that the split-dollar equity is taxable and subject to Section 409A. The purpose of the Notice was to establish a transition rule for amending grandfathered split-dollar regulation arrangements to meet the provisions of Section 409A without constituting a material modification that would lose the grandfathering from the Final Split-Dollar Regulations.[372] The Notice states that the arrangements grandfathered from the Regulations provide deferred compensation if, under the terms of the arrangement and the relevant facts and circumstances, "the service provider has a legally binding right during a taxable year to compensation that pursuant to the terms of the arrangement is payable to . . . the service provider in a later year (for example, upon termination of the split-dollar arrangement)."[373] The Notice does not speak of equity split-dollar but that has to be what is being referenced. Thus, the implication that Section 409A might apply to the equity in a split-dollar regulation grandfathered arrangement that is not also grandfathered from the Section 409A regulations.

The bottom line seems to be that under Notice 2007-34, Section 409A does not apply to Final Split-Dollar Regulations grandfathered equity arrangements if they are also grandfathered from the Section 409A final regulations (e.g., earned and vested on December 31, 2004) or as long as the arrangement has not been terminated during the life of the insured and the economic benefit of the cost of current life insurance is either being paid by the employee to the employer or is included in the employee's W-2. It is unclear whether or when Section 409A might apply at the termination of a Final Split-Dollar Regulations grandfathered arrangement that is not grandfathered under the Section 409A final regulations (e.g., premium payments made by the employer after 2004 which are themselves subject to a substantial risk of forfeiture).

Without authority on the issue, there are three theories: (1) if the equity is subject to tax under Section 83 (because "no inference" is held not to prevent taxation), Section 409A applies; (2) if the equity is not taxed under Section 83 (because of the "no inference" language), Section 409A still applies by itself (because it doesn't contain the "no inference" language); and (3) if the equity is not taxable under Section 83, Section 409A does not apply (if the "no inference" language applies).

VIII. Conclusion

With the effective date of the Final Split-Dollar Regulations in 2003, many commentators asserted that split-dollar premium financing was dead. A reader of this book should be persuaded that these predictions were indeed premature. Although split-dollar arrangements have significantly changed from the grandfathered split-dollar rules (although in many ways they have remained the same), such arrangements are very much alive today; they are not dead but merely different.

The loan regime is perhaps the most prevalent form of split-dollar premium financing. In almost every case when money is borrowed to pay premiums, parties are involved in a loan regime transaction (whether they realize it or not). In fact, the Final Split-Dollar Regulations boost the popularity of the loan regime by in effect blessing equity split-dollar arrangements, favoring the owner at the cost of paying the AFR. Gone is the uncertainty as to the income and gift tax consequences of grandfathered equity split-dollar arrangements. The loan regime is favored in financing cross-purchase agreements and providing for wealth transfer, and it is often used in connection with deferred compensation arrangements.

Although not as popular as the loan regime, the economic benefit regime fills certain niches in giving the premium payer control over the policy and its cash value. It is useful for some executive deferred compensation arrangements and for providing death benefits by an employer to the beneficiaries of an employee. It is especially useful for arrangements involving survivorship policies because of the low economic benefit costs that are available while both insureds are alive. Both regimes can be used to provide inexpensive life insurance coverage to an executive.

Particularly with premium loans, practitioners (to their peril) may not realize that they are involved with the split-dollar regimes when financing life insurance premium payments. Hopefully, this book will serve as a useful guide in providing for leveraging life insurance premium payments, whichever regime is used.

Appendix 1

Table 2001

Interim Table of 1-Year Term Premiums for $1,000 of Life Insurance Protection

Attained Age	Section 79 Extended and Interpolated Annual Rates	Attained Age	Section 79 Extended and Interpolated Annual Rates	Attained Age	Section 79 Extended and Interpolated Annual Rates
0	0.70	35	$0.99	70	$20.62
1	$0.41	36	$1.01	71	322.72
2	$0.27	37	$1.04	72	$25.07
3	$0.19	38	$1.06	73	$27.57
4	$0.13	39	$1.07	74	$30.18
5	$0.13	40	$1.10	75	$33.05
6	$0.14	41	$1.13	76	$36.33
7	$0.15	42	$1.20	77	$40.17
8	$0.16	43	$1.29	78	$44.33
9	$0.16	44	$1.40	79	$49.23
10	$0.16	45	$1.53	80	$54.56
11	$0.19	46	$1.67	81	$60.51
12	$0.24	47	$1.83	82	$66.74
13	$0.28	48	$1.98	83	$73.07
14	$0.33	49	$2.13	84	$80.35
15	$0.38	50	$2.30	85	$88.76
16	$0.52	51	$2.52	86	$99.16
17	$0.57	52	$2.81	87	$110.40
18	$0.59	53	$3.20	88	$121.85
19	$0.61	54	$3.65	89	$133.40
20	$0.62	55	$4.15	90	$144.30
21	$0.62	56	$4.68	91	$155.80
22	$0.64	57	$5.20	92	$168.75
23	$0.66	58	$5.66	93	$186.44
24	$0.68	59	$6.06	94	$206.70
25	$0.71	60	$6.51	95	$228.35
26	$0.73	61	$7.11	96	$250.01
27	$0.76	62	$7.96	97	$265.09
28	$0.80	63	$9.08	98	$270.11
29	$0.83	64	$10.41	99	$281.05
30	$0.87	65	$11.90		
31	$0.90	66	$13.51		
32	$0.93	67	$15.20		
33	$0.96	68	$16.92		
34	$0.98	69	$18.70		

Appendix 2

Comparison of Table of Term Rates

Comparison Table of Term Rates at Selected Ages (Per $1,000 of Insurance)

Age(s)	PS58 (obsolete)	Table 2001	One Carrier's Alternative Term Rate	Survivorship Rate*
50	9.22	2.30	.79	.01
55	13.74	4.55	1.08	.02
60	20.73	6.51	1.77	.04
65	31.51	11.90	2.75	.14
70	48.06	20.62	4.52	.43
75	83.23	33.05	7.05	1.09
80	111.04	54.56	11.95	2.98

* Assumes both insureds are the same age.

Appendix 3

Table 2001 Joint and Survivor Term Rates

Table 2001 Joint and Survivor Term Rates per $1,000 of Insurance

Ages	49	50	51	52	53	54	55	56	57	58	59	60	61	62	63	64	65	66	67	68
49	$0.00	$0.00	$0.01	$0.01	$0.01	$0.01	$0.01	$0.01	$0.01	$0.01	$0.01	$0.01	$0.02	$0.02	$0.02	$0.02	$0.03	$0.03	$0.03	$0.04
50	$0.00	$0.01	$0.01	$0.01	$0.01	$0.01	$0.01	$0.01	$0.01	$0.01	$0.01	$0.01	$0.02	$0.02	$0.02	$0.02	$0.03	$0.03	$0.03	$0.04
51	$0.01	$0.01	$0.01	$0.01	$0.01	$0.01	$0.01	$0.01	$0.01	$0.01	$0.02	$0.02	$0.02	$0.02	$0.02	$0.03	$0.03	$0.03	$0.04	$0.04
52	$0.01	$0.01	$0.01	$0.01	$0.01	$0.01	$0.01	$0.01	$0.01	$0.02	$0.02	$0.02	$0.02	$0.02	$0.03	$0.03	$0.03	$0.04	$0.04	$0.05
53	$0.01	$0.01	$0.01	$0.01	$0.01	$0.01	$0.01	$0.01	$0.02	$0.02	$0.02	$0.02	$0.02	$0.03	$0.03	$0.03	$0.04	$0.04	$0.05	$0.05
54	$0.01	$0.01	$0.01	$0.01	$0.01	$0.01	$0.02	$0.02	$0.02	$0.02	$0.02	$0.02	$0.03	$0.03	$0.03	$0.04	$0.04	$0.05	$0.06	$0.06
55	$0.01	$0.01	$0.01	$0.01	$0.01	$0.02	$0.02	$0.02	$0.02	$0.02	$0.03	$0.03	$0.03	$0.03	$0.04	$0.04	$0.05	$0.06	$0.06	$0.07
56	$0.01	$0.01	$0.01	$0.01	$0.01	$0.02	$0.02	$0.02	$0.02	$0.03	$0.03	$0.03	$0.03	$0.04	$0.04	$0.05	$0.06	$0.06	$0.07	$0.08
57	$0.01	$0.01	$0.01	$0.01	$0.02	$0.02	$0.02	$0.02	$0.03	$0.03	$0.03	$0.03	$0.04	$0.04	$0.05	$0.05	$0.06	$0.07	$0.08	$0.09
58	$0.01	$0.01	$0.01	$0.02	$0.02	$0.02	$0.02	$0.03	$0.03	$0.03	$0.03	$0.04	$0.04	$0.05	$0.05	$0.06	$0.07	$0.08	$0.09	$0.10
59	$0.01	$0.01	$0.02	$0.02	$0.02	$0.02	$0.03	$0.03	$0.03	$0.03	$0.04	$0.04	$0.04	$0.05	$0.06	$0.06	$0.07	$0.08	$0.09	$0.10
60	$0.01	$0.01	$0.02	$0.02	$0.02	$0.02	$0.03	$0.03	$0.03	$0.04	$0.04	$0.04	$0.05	$0.05	$0.06	$0.07	$0.08	$0.09	$0.10	$0.11
61	$0.02	$0.02	$0.02	$0.02	$0.02	$0.03	$0.03	$0.03	$0.04	$0.04	$0.04	$0.05	$0.05	$0.06	$0.06	$0.07	$0.08	$0.10	$0.11	$0.12
62	$0.02	$0.02	$0.02	$0.02	$0.03	$0.03	$0.03	$0.04	$0.04	$0.05	$0.05	$0.05	$0.06	$0.06	$0.07	$0.08	$0.09	$0.11	$0.12	$0.13
63	$0.02	$0.02	$0.02	$0.03	$0.03	$0.03	$0.04	$0.04	$0.05	$0.05	$0.06	$0.06	$0.06	$0.07	$0.08	$0.09	$0.11	$0.12	$0.14	$0.15
64	$0.02	$0.02	$0.03	$0.03	$0.03	$0.04	$0.04	$0.05	$0.05	$0.06	$0.06	$0.07	$0.07	$0.08	$0.09	$0.11	$0.12	$0.14	$0.16	$0.18
65	$0.03	$0.03	$0.03	$0.03	$0.04	$0.04	$0.05	$0.06	$0.06	$0.07	$0.07	$0.08	$0.08	$0.09	$0.11	$0.12	$0.14	$0.16	$0.18	$0.20
66	$0.03	$0.03	$0.03	$0.04	$0.04	$0.05	$0.06	$0.06	$0.07	$0.08	$0.08	$0.09	$0.10	$0.11	$0.12	$0.14.	$0.16	$0.18	$0.21	$0.23
67	$0.03	$0.03	$0.04	$0.04	$0.05	$0.06	$0.06	$0.07	$0.08	$0.09	$0.09	$0.10	$0.11	$0.12	$0.14	$0.16	$0.18	$0.21	$0.23	$0.26
68	$0.04	$0.04	$0.04	$0.05	$0.05	$0.06	$0.07	$0.08	$0.09	$0.10	$0.10	$0.11	$0.12	$0.13	$0.15	$0.18	$0.20	$0.23	$0.26	$0.29
69	$0.04	$0.04	$0.05	$0.05	$0.06	$0.07	$0.08	$0.09	$0.10	$0.11	$0.11	$0.12	$0.13	$0.15	$0.17	$0.19	$0.22	$0.25	$0.28	$0.32
70	$0.04	$0.05	$0.05	$0.06	$0.07	$0.08	$0.09	$0.10	$0.11	$0.12	$0.12	$0.13	$0.15	$0.16	$0.19	$0.21	$0.25	$0.28	$0.31	$0.35
71	$0.05	$0.05	$0.06	$0.06	$0.07	$0.08	$0.09	$0.11	$0.12	$0.13	$0.14	$0.15	$0.16	$0.18	$0.21	$0.24	$0.27	$0.31	$0.35	$0.38

(Continued)

Ages	49	50	51	52	53	54	55	56	57	58	59	60	61	62	63	64	65	66	67	68
72	$0.05	$0.06	$0.06	$0.07	$0.08	$0.09	$0.10	$0.12	$0.13	$0.14	$0.15	$0.16	$0.18	$0.20	$0.23	$0.26	$0.30	$0.34	$0.38	$0.42
73	$0.06	$0.06	$0.07	$0.08	$0.09	$0.10	$0.11	$0.13	$0.14	$0.16	$0.17	$0.18	$0.20	$0.22	$0.25	$0.29	$0.33	$0.37	$0.42	$0.47
74	$0.06	$0.07	$0.08	$0.08	$0.10	$0.11	$0.13	$0.14	$0.16	$0.17	$0.18	$0.20	$0.21	$0.24	$0.27	$0.31	$0.36	$0.41	$0.46	$0.51
75	$0.07	$0.08	$0.08	$0.09	$0.11	$0.12	$0.14	$0.15	$0.17	$0.19	$0.20	$0.22	$0.23	$0.26	$0.30	$0.34	$0.39	$0.45	$0.50	$0.56
76	$0.08	$0.08	$0.09	$0.10	$0.12	$0.13	$0.15	$0.17	$0.19	$0.21	$0.22	$0.24	$0.26	$0.29	$0.33	$0.38	$0.43	$0.49	$0.55	$0.61
77	$0.09	$0.09	$0.10	$0.11	$0.13	$0.15	$0.17	$0.19	$0.21	$0.23	$0.24	$0.26	$0.29	$0.32	$0.36	$0.42	$0.48	$0.54	$0.61	$0.68
78	$0.09	$0.10	$0.11	$0.12	$0.14	$0.16	$0.18	$0.21	$0.23	$0.25	$0.27	$0.29	$0.32	$0.35	$0.40	$0.46	$0.53	$0.60	$0.67	$0.75
79	$0.10	$0.11	$0.12	$0.14	$0.16	$0.18	$0.20	$0.23	$0.26	$0.28	$0.30	$0.32	$0.35	$0.39	$0.45	$0.51	$0.59	$0.67	$0.75	$0.83
80	$0.12	$0.13	$0.14	$0.15	$0.17	$0.20	$0.23	$0.26	$0.28	$0.31	$0.33	$0.36	$0.39	$0.43	$0.50	$0.57	$0.65	$0.74	$0.83	$0.92
81	$0.13	$0.14	$0.15	$0.17	$0.19	$0.22	$0.25	$0.28	$0.31	$0.34	$0.37	$0.39	$0.43	$0.48	$0.55	$0.63	$0.72	$0.82	$0.92	$1.02
82	$0.14	$0.15	$0.17	$0.19	$0.21	$0.24	$0.28	$0.31	$0.35	$0.38	$0.40	$0.43	$0.47	$0.53	$0.61	$0.69	$0.79	$0.90	$1.01	$1.13
83	$0.16	$0.17	$0.18	$0.21	$0.23	$0.27	$0.30	$0.34	$0.38	$0.41	$0.44	$0.48	$0.52	$0.58	$0.66	$0.76	$0.87	$0.99	$1.11	$1.24
84	$0.17	$0.18	$0.20	$0.23	$0.26	$0.29	$0.33	$0.38	$0.42	$0.45	$0.49	$0.52	$0.57	$0.64	$0.73	$0.84	$0.96	$1.09	$1.22	$1.36
85	$0.19	$0.20	$0.22	$0.25	$0.28	$0.32	$0.37	$0.42	$0.46	$0.50	$0.54	$0.58	$0.63	$0.71	$0.81	$0.92	$1.06	$1.20	$1.35	$1.50
86	$0.21	$0.23	$0.25	$0.28	$0.32	$0.36	$0.41	$0.46	$0.52	$0.56	$0.60	$0.65	$0.71	$0.79	$0.90	$1.03	$1.18	$1.34	$1.51	$1.68
87	$0.24	$0.25	$0.28	$0.31	$0.35	$0.40	$0.46	$0.52	$0.57	$0.62	$0.67	$0.72	$0.78	$0.88	$1.00	$1.15	$1.31	$1.49	$1.68	$1.87
88	$0.26	$0.28	$0.31	$0.34	$0.39	$0.44	$0.51	$0.57	$0.63	$0.69	$0.74	$0.79	$0.87	$0.97	$1.11	$1.27	$1.45	$1.65	$1.85	$2.06
89	$0.28	$0.31	$0.34	$0.37	$0.43	$0.49	$0.55	$0.62	$0.69	$0.76	$0.81	$0.87	$0.95	$1.06	$1.21	$1.39	$1.59	$1.80	$2.03	$2.26
90	$0.31	$0.33	$0.36	$0.41	$0.46	$0.53	$0.60	$0.68	$0.75	$0.82	$0.87	$0.94	$1.03	$1.15	$1.31	$1.50	$1.72	$1.95	$2.19	$2.44
91	$0.33	$0.36	$0.39	$0.44	$0.50	$0.57	$0.65	$0.73	$0.81	$0.88	$0.94	$1.01	$1.11	$1.24	$1.41	$1.62	$1.85	$2.10	$2.37	$2.64
92	$0.36	$0.39	$0.43	$0.47	$0.54	$0.62	$0.70	$0.79	$0.88	$0.96	$1.02	$1.10	$1.20	$1.34	$1.53	$1.76	$2.01	$2.28	$2.57	$2.86
93	$0.40	$0.43	$0.47	$0.52	$0.60	$0.68	$0.77	$0.87	$0.97	$1.06	$1.13	$1.21	$1.33	$1.48	$1.69	$1.94	$2.22	$2.52	$2.83	$3.15
94	$0.44	$0.48	$0.52	$0.58	$0.66	$0.75	$0.86	$0.97	$1.07	$1.17	$1.25	$1.35	$1.47	$1.65	$1.88	$2.15	$2.46	$2.79	$3.14	$3.50
95	$0.49	$0.53	$0.58	$0.64	$0.73	$0.83	$0.95	$1.07	$1.19	$1.29	$1.38	$1.49	$1.62	$1.82	$2.07	$2.38	$2.72	$3.09	$3.47	$3.86
96	$0.53	$0.58	$0.63	$0.70	$0.80	$0.91	$1.04	$1.17	$1.30	$1.42	$1.52	$1.63	$1.78	$1.99	$2.27	$2.60	$2.98	$3.38	$3.80	$4.23
97	$0.56	$0.61	$0.67	$0.74	$0.85	$0.97	$1.10	$1.24	$1.38	$1.50	$1.61	$1.73	$1.88	$2.11	$2.41	$2.76	$3.15	$3.58	$4.03	$4.49
98	$0.58	$0.62	$0.68	$0.76	$0.86	$0.99	$1.12	$1.26	$1.40	$1.53	$1.64	$1.76	$1.92	$2.15	$2.45	$2.81	$3.21	$3.65	$4.11	$4.57
99	$0.60	$0.65	$0.71	$0.79	$0.90	$1.03	$1.17	$1.32	$1.46	$1.59	$1.70	$1.83	$2.00	$2.24	$2.55	$2.93	$3.34	$3.80	$4.27	$4.76

Ages	69	70	71	72	73	74	75	76	77	78	79	80	81	82	83	84	85	86
49	$0.04	$0.04	$0.05	$0.05	$0.06	$0.06	$0.07	$0.08	$0.09	$0.09	$0.10	$0.12	$0.13	$0.14	$0.16	$0.17	$0.19	$0.21
50	$0.04	$0.05	$0.05	$0.06	$0.06	$0.07	$0.08	$0.08	$0.09	$0.10	$0.11	$0.13	$0.14	$0.15	$0.17	$0.18	$0.20	$0.23
51	$0.05	$0.05	$0.06	$0.06	$0.07	$0.08	$0.08	$0.09	$0.10	$0.11	$0.12	$0.14	$0.15	$0.17	$0.18	$0.20	$0.22	$0.25
52	$0.05	$0.06	$0.06	$0.07	$0.08	$0.08	$0.09	$0.10	$0.11	$0.12	$0.14	$0.15	$0.17	$0.19	$0.21	$0.23	$0.25	$0.28
53	$0.06	$0.07	$0.07	$0.08	$0.09	$0.10	$0.11	$0.12	$0.13	$0.14	$0.16	$0.17	$0.19	$0.21	$0.23	$0.26	$0.28	$0.32
54	$0.07	$0.08	$0.08	$0.09	$0.10	$0.11	$0.12	$0.13	$0.15	$0.16	$0.18	$0.20	$0.22	$0.24	$0.27	$0.29	$0.32	$0.36
55	$0.08	$0.09	$0.09	$0.10	$0.11	$0.13	$0.14	$0.15	$0.17	$0.18	$0.20	$0.23	$0.25	$0.28	$0.30	$0.33	$0.37	$0.41
56	$0.09	$0.10	$0.11	$0.12	$0.13	$0.14	$0.15	$0.17	$0.19	$0.21	$0.23	$0.26	$0.28	$0.31	$0.34	$0.38	$0.42	$0.46
57	$0.10	$0.11	$0.12	$0.13	$0.14	$0.16	$0.17	$0.19	$0.21	$0.23	$0.26	$0.28	$0.31	$0.35	$0.38	$0.42	$0.46	$0.52
58	$0.11	$0.12	$0.13	$0.14	$0.16	$0.17	$0.19	$0.21	$0.23	$0.25	$0.28	$0.31	$0.34	$0.38	$0.41	$0.45	$0.50	$0.56
59	$0.11	$0.12	$0.14	$0.15	$0.17	$0.18	$0.20	$0.22	$0.24	$0.27	$0.30	$0.33	$0.37	$0.40	$0.44	$0.49	$0.54	$0.60
60	$0.12	$0.13	$0.15	$0.16	$0.18	$0.20	$0.22	$0.24	$0.26	$0.29	$0.32	$0.36	$0.39	$0.43	$0.48	$0.52	$0.58	$0.65
61	$0.13	$0.15	$0.16	$0.18	$0.20	$0.21	$0.23	$0.26	$0.29	$0.32	$0.35	$0.39	$0.43	$0.47	$0.52	$0.57	$0.63	$0.71
62	$0.15	$0.16	$0.18	$0.20	$0.22	$0.24	$0.26	$0.29	$0.32	$0.35	$0.39	$0.43	$0.48	$0.53	$0.58	$0.64	$0.71	$0.79
63	$0.17	$0.19	$0.21	$0.23	$0.25	$0.27	$0.30	$0.33	$0.36	$0.40	$0.45	$0.50	$0.55	$0.61	$0.66	$0.73	$0.81	$0.90
64	$0.19	$0.21	$0.24	$0.26	$0.29	$0.31	$0.34	$0.38	$0.42	$0.46	$0.51	$0.57	$0.63	$0.69	$0.76	$0.84	$0.92	$1.03
65	$0.22	$0.25	$0.27	$0.30	$0.33	$0.36	$0.39	$0.43	$0.48	$0.53	$0.59	$0.65	$0.72	$0.79	$0.87	$0.96	$1.06	$1.18
66	$0.25	$0.28	$0.31	$0.34	$0.37	$0.41	$0.45	$0.49	$0.54	$0.60	$0.67	$0.74	$0.82	$0.90	$0.99	$1.09	$1.20	$1.34
67	$0.28	$0.31	$0.35	$0.38	$0.42	$0.46	$0.50	$0.55	$0.61	$0.67	$0.75	$0.83	$0.92	$1.01	$1.11	$1.22	$1.35	$1.51
68	$0.32	$0.35	$0.38	$0.42	$0.47	$0.51	$0.56	$0.61	$0.68	$0.75	$0.83	$0.92	$1.02	$1.13	$1.24	$1.36	$1.50	$1.68
69	$0.35	$0.39	$0.42	$0.47	$0.52	$0.56	$0.62	$0.68	$0.75	$0.83	$0.92	$1.02	$1.13	$1.25	$1.37	$1.50	$1.66	$1.85
70	$0.39	$0.43	$0.47	$0.52	$0.57	$0.62	$0.68	$0.75	$0.83	$0.91	$1.02	$1.13	$1.25	$1.38	$1.51	$1.66	$1.83	$2.04
71	$0.42	$0.47	$0.52	$0.57	$0.63	$0.69	$0.75	$0.83	$0.91	$1.01	$1.12	$1.24	$1.37	$1.52	$1.66	$1.83	$2.02	$2.25
72	$0.47	$0.52	$0.57	$0.63	$0.69	$0.76	$0.83	$0.91	$1.01	$1.11	$1.23	$1.37	$1.52	$1.67	$1.83	$2.01	$2.23	$2.49
73	$0.52	$0.57	$0.63	$0.69	$0.76	$0.83	$0.91	$1.00	$1.11	$1.22	$1.36	$1.50	$1.67	$1.84	$2.01	$2.22	$2.45	$2.73
74	$0.56	$0.62	$0.69	$0.76	$0.83	$0.91	$1.00	$1.10	$1.21	$1.34	$1.49	$1.65	$1.83	$2.01	$2.21	$2.42	$2.68	$2.99

(Continued)

Ages	69	70	71	72	73	74	75	76	77	78	79	80	81	82	83	84	85	86
75	$0.62	$0.68	$0.75	$0.83	$0.91	$1.00	$1.09	$1.20	$1.33	$1.47	$1.63	$1.80	$2.00	$2.21	$2.41	$2.66	$2.93	$3.28
76	$0.68	$0.75	$0.83	$0.91	$1.00	$1.10	$1.20	$1.32	$1.46	$1.61	$1.79	$1.98	$2.20	$2.42	$2.65	$2.92	$3.22	$3.60
77	$0.75	$0.83	$0.91	$1.01	$1.11	$1.21	$1.33	$1.46	$1.61	$1.78	$1.98	$2.19	$2.43	$2.68	$2.94	$3.23	$3.57	$3.98
78	$0.83	$0.91	$1.01	$1.11	$1.22	$1.34	$1.47	$1.61	$1.78	$1.97	$2.18	$2.42	$2.68	$2.96	$3.24	$3.56	$3.93	$4.40
79	$0.92	$1.02	$1.12	$1.23	$1.36	$1.49	$1.63	$1.79	$1.98	$2.18	$2.42	$2.69	$2.98	$3.29	$3.60	$3.96	$4.37	$4.88
80	$1.02	$1.13	$1.24	$1.37	$1.50	$1.65	$1.80	$1.98	$2.19	$2.42	$2.69	$2.98	$3.30	$3.64	$3.99	$4.38	$4.84	$5.41
81	$1.13	$1.25	$1.37	$1.52	$1.67	$1.83	$2.00	$2.20	$2.43	$2.68	$2.98	$3.30	$3.66	$4.04	$4.42	$486	$5.37	$6.00
82	$1.25	$1.38	$1.52	$1.67	$1.84	$2.01	$2.21	$2.42	$2.68	$2.96	$3.29	$3.64	$4.04	$4.45	$4.88	$5.36	$5.92	$6.62
83	$1.37	$1.51	$1.66	$1.83	$2.01	$2.21	$2.41	$2.65	$2.94	$3.24	$3.60	$3.99	$4.42	$4.88	$5.34	$5.87	$6.49	$7.25
84	$1.50	$1.66	$1.83	$2.01	$2.22	$2.42	$2.66	$2.92	$3.23	$3.56	$3.96	$4.38	$4.86	$5.36	$5.87	$6.46	$7.13	$7.97
85	$1.66	$1.83	$2.02	$2.23	$2.45	$2.68	$2.93	$3.22	$3.57	$3.93	$4.37	$4.84	$5.37	$5.92	$6.49	$7.13	$7.88	$8.80
86	$1.85	$2.04	$2.25	$2.49	$2.73	$2.99	$3.28	$3.60	$3.98	$4.40	$4.88	$5.41	$6.00	$6.62	$7.25	$7.97	$8.80	$9.83
87	$2.06	$2.28	$2.51	$2.77	$3.04	$3.33	$3.65	$4.01	$4.43	$4.89	$5.43	$6.02	$6.68	$7.37	$8.07	$8.87	$9.80	$10.95
88	$2.28	$2.51	$2.77	$3.05	$3.36	$3.68	$4.03	$4.43	$4.89	$5.40	$6.00	$6.65	$7.37	$8.13	$8.90	$9.79	$10.82	$12.08
89	$2.49	$2.75	$3.03	$3.34	$3.68	$4.03	$4.41	$4.85	$5.36	$5.91	$6.57	$7.28	$8.07	$8.90	$9.75	$10.72	$11.84	$13.23
90	$2.70	$2.98	$3.28	$3.62	$3.98	$4.35	$4.77	$5.24	$5.80	$6.40	$7.10	$7.87	$8.73	$9.63	$10.54	$11.59	$12.81	$14.31
91	$2.91	$3.21	$3.54	$3.91	$4.30	$4.70	$5.15	$5.66	$6.26	$6.91	$7.67	$8.50	$9.43	$10.40	$11.38	$12.52	$13.83	$15.45
92	$3.16	$3.48	$3.83	$4.23	$4.65	$5.09	$5.58	$6.13	$6.78	$7.48	$8.31	$9.21	$10.21	$11.26	$12.33	$13.56	$14.98	$16.73
93	$3.49	$3.84	$4.24	$4.67	$5.14	$5.63	$6.16	$6.77	$7.49	$8.26	$9.18	$10.17	$11.28	$12.44	$13.62	$14.98	$16.55	$18.49
94	$3.87	$4..26	$4.70	$5.18	$5.70	$6.24	$6.83	$7.51	$8.30	$9.16	$10.18	$11.28	$12.51	$13.80	$15.10	$16.61	$18.35	$20.50
95	$4.27	$4.71	$5.19	$5.72	$6.30	$6.89	$7.55	$8.30	$9.17	$10.12	$11.24	$12.46	$13.82	$15.24	$16.69	$18.35	$20.27	$22.64
96	$4.68	$5.16	$5.68	$6.27	$6.89	$7.55	$8.26	$9.08	$10.04	$11.08	$12.31	$13.64	$15.13	$16.69	$18.27	$20.09	$22.19	$24.79
97	$4.96	$5.47	$6.02	$6.65	$7.31	$8.00	$8.76	$9.63	$10.65	$11.75	$13.05	$14.46	$16.04	$17.69	$19.37	$21.30	$23.53	$26.29
98	$5.05	$5.57	$6.14	$6.77	$7.45	$8.15	$8.93	$9.81	$10.85	$11.97	$13.30	$14.74	$16.34	$18.03	$19.74	$21.70	$23.97	$26.78
99	$5.26	$5.80	$6.39	$7.05	$7.75	$8.48	$9.29	$10.21	$11.29	$12.46	$13.84	$15.33	$17.01	$18.76	$20.54	$22.58	$24.95	$27.87

Ages	87	88	89	90	91	92	93	94	95	96	97	98	99
49	$0.24	$0.26	$0.28	$0.31	$0.33	$0.36	$0.40	$0.44	$0.49	$0.53	$0.56	$0.58	$0.60
50	$0.25	$0.28	$0.31	$0.33	$0.36	$0.39	$0.43	$0.48	$0.53	$0.58	$0.61	$0.62	$0.65
51	$0.28	$0.31	$0.34	$0.36	$0.39	$0.43	$0.47	$0.52	$0.58	$0.63	$0.67	$0.68	$0.71
52	$0.31	$0.34	$0.37	$0.41	$0.44	$0.47	$0.52	$0.58	$0.64	$0.70	$0.74	$0.76	$0.79
53	$0.35	$0.39	$0.43	$0.46	$0.50	$0.54	$0.60	$0.66	$0.73	$0.80	$0.85	$0.86	$0.90
54	$0.40	$0.44	$0.49	$0.53	$0.57	$0.62	$0.68	$0.75	$0.83	$0.91	$0.97	$0.99	$1.03
55	$0.46	$0.51	$0.55	$0.60	$0.65	$0.70	$0.77	$0.86	$0.95	$1.04	$1.10	$1.12	$1.17
56	$0.52	$0.57	$0.62	$0.68	$0.73	$0.79	$0.87	$0.97	$1.07	$1.17	$1.24	$1.26	$1.32
57	$0.57	$0.63	$0.69	$0.75	$0.81	$0.88	$0.97	$1.07	$1.19	$1.30	$1.38	$1.40	$1.46
58	$0.62	$0.69	$0.76	$0.82	$0.88	$0.96	$1.06	$1.17	$1.29	$1.42	$1.50	$1.53	$1.59
59	$0.67	$0.74	$0.81	$0.87	$0.94	$1.02	$1.13	$1.25	$1.38	$1.52	$1.61	$1.64	$1.70
60	$0.72	$0.79	$0.87	$0.94	$1.01	$1.10	$1.21	$1.35	$1.49	$1.63	$1.73	$1.76	$1.83
61	$0.78	$0.87	$0.95	$1.03	$1.11	$1.20	$1.33	$1.47	$1.62	$1.78	$1.88	$1.92	$2.00
62	$0.88	$0.97	$1.06	$1.15	$1.24	$1.34	$1.48	$1.65	$1.82	$1.99	$2.11	$2.15	$2.24
63	$1.00	$1.11	$1.21	$1.31	$1.41	$1.53	$1.69	$1.88	$2.07	$2.27	$2.41	$2.45	$2.55
64	$1.15	$1.27	$1.39	$1.50	$1.62	$1.76	$1.94	$2.15	$2.38	$2.60	$2.76	$2.81	$2.93
65	$1.31	$1.45	$1.59	$1.72	$1.85	$2.01	$2.22	$2.46	$2.72	$2.98	$3.15	$3.21	$3.34
66	$1.49	$1.65	$1.80	$1.95	$2.10	$2.28	$2.52	$2.79	$3.09	$3.38	$3.58	$3.65	$3.80
67	$1.68	$1.85	$2.03	$2.19	$2.37	$2.57	$2.83	$3.14	$3.47	$3.80	$4.03	$4.11	$4.27
68	$1.87	$2.06	$2.26	$2.44	$2.64	$2.86	$3.15	$3.50	$3.86	$4.23	$4.49	$4.57	$4.76
69	$2.06	$2.28	$2.49	$2.70	$2.91	$3.16	$3.49	$3.87	$4.27	$4.68	$4.96	$5.05	$5.26
70	$2.28	$2.51	$2.75	$2.98	$3.21	$3.48	$3.84	$4.26	$4.71	$5.16	$5.47	$5.57	$5.80
71	$2.51	$2.77	$3.03	$3.28	$3.54	$3.83	$4.24	$4.70	$5.19	$5.68	$6.02	$6.14	$6.39
72	$2.77	$3.05	$3.34	$3.62	$3.91	$4.23	$4.67	$5.18	$5.72	$6.27	$6.65	$6.77	$7.05
73	$3.04	$3.36	$3.68	$3.98	$430	$4.65	$5.14	$5.70	$6.30	$6.89	$7.31	$7.45	$7.75
74	$3.33	$3.68	$4.03	$4.35	$4.70	$5.09	$5.63	$6.24	$6.89	$7.55	$8.00	$8.15	$8.48

(Continued)

Ages	87	88	89	90	91	92	93	94	95	96	97	98	99
75	$3.65	$4.03	$4.41	$4.77	$5.15	$5.58	$6.16	$6.83	$7.55	$8.26	$8.76	$8.93	$9.29
76	$4.01	$4.43	$4.85	$5.24	$5.66	$6.13	$6.77	$7.51	$8.30	$9.08	$9.63	$9.81	$10.21
77	$4.43	$4.89	$5.36	$5.80	$6.26	$6.78	$7.49	$8.30	$9.17	$10.04	$10.65	$10.85	$11.29
78	$4.89	$5.40	$5.91	$6.40	$6.91	$7.48	$8.26	$9.16	$10.12	$11.08	$11.75	$11.97	$12.46
79	$5.43	$6.00	$6.57	$7.10	$7.67	$8.31	$9.18	$10.18	$11.24	$12.31	$13.05	$13.30	$13.84
80	$6.02	$6.65	$7.28	$7.87	$8.50	$9.21	$10.17	$11.28	$12.46	$13.64	$14.46	$14.74	$15.33
81	$6.68	$7.37	$8.07	$8.73	$9.43	$10.21	$11.28	$12.51	$13.82	$15.13	$16.04	$16.34	$17.01
82	$7.37	$8.13	$8.90	$9.63	$10.40	$11.26	$12.44	$13.80	$15.24	$16.69	$17.69	$18.03	$18.76
83	$8.07	$8.90	$9.75	$10.54	$11.38	$12.33	$13.62	$15.10	$16.69	$18.27	$19.37	$19.74	$20.54
84	$8.87	$9.79	$10.72	$11.59	$12.52	$13.56	$14.98	$16.61	$18.35	$20.09	$21.30	$21.70	$22.58
85	$9.80	$10.82	$11.84	$12.81	$13.83	$14.98	$16.55	$18.35	$20.27	$22.19	$23.53	$23.97	$24.95
86	$10.95	$12.08	$13.23	$14.31	$15.45	$16.73	$18.49	$20.50	$22.64	$24.79	$26.29	$26.78	$27.87
87	$12.19	$13.45	$14.73	$15.93	$17.20	$18.63	$20.58	$22.82	$25.21	$27.60	$29.27	$29.82	$31.03
88	$13.45	$14.85	$16.25	$17.58	$18.98	$20.56	$22.72	$25.19	$27.82	$30.46	$32.30	$32.91	$34.25
89	$14.73	$16.25	$17.80	$19.25	$20.78	$22.51	$24.87	$27.57	$30.46	$33.35	$35.36	$36.03	$37.49
90	$15.93	$17.58	$19.25	$20.82	$22.48	$24.35	$26.90	$29.83	$32.95	$36.08	$38.25	$38.98	$40.56
91	$17.20	$18.98	$20.78	$22.48	$24.27	$26.29	$29.05	$32.20	$35.58	$38.95	$41.30	$42.08	$43.79
92	$18.63	$20.56	$22.51	$24.35	$26.29	$28.48	$31.46	$34.88	$38.53	$42.19	$44.73	$45.58	$47.43
93	$20.58	$22.72	$24.87	$26.90	$29.05	$31.46	$34.76	$38.54	$42.57	$46.61	$49.42	$50.36	$52.40
94	$22.82	$25.19	$27.57	$29.83	$32.20	$34.88	$38.54	$42.72	$47.20	$51.68	$54.79	$55.83	$58.09
95	$25.21	$27.82	$30.46	$32.95	$35.58	$38.53	$42.57	$47.20	$52.14	$57.09	$60.53	$61.68	$64.18
96	$27.60	$30.46	$33.35	$36.08	$38.95	$42.19	$46.61	$51.68	$57.09	$62.51	$66.28	$67.53	$70.27
97	$29.27	$32.30	$35.36	$38.25	$41.30	$44.73	$49.42	$54.79	$60.53	$66.28	$70.27	$71.60	$74.50
98	$29.82	$32.91	$36.03	$38.98	$42.08	$45.58	$50.36	$55.83	$61.68	$67.53	$71.60	$72.96	$75.91
99	$31.03	$34.25	$37.49	$40.56	$43.79	$47.43	$52.40	$58.09	$64.18	$70.27	$74.50	$75.91	$78.99

Endnotes

1 Treas. Reg. Sec. 1.7872-15.

2 Treas. Reg. Secs. 1.61-22(d) through (g).

3 Treas. Reg. Sec. 1.7872-5T(b)(1).

4 Defined in Section 1274(d) and set monthly by the Secretary of Treasury for short- term, mid-term, and long-term rates for debt instruments.

5 Treas. Reg. Sec. 1.61-22(b)(1).

6 "Permanent benefit" is defined as an economic value extending beyond 1 policy year. Treas. Reg. Sec. 1.79-0.

7 Treas. Reg. Sec. 1.61-22(b)(2).

8 Our Country Home Enterprises, Inc. v. Commissioner, 145 T.C. 1 (2015). De Los Santos v. Commissioner, T.C. Memo 2018-155 (2018) Machacek v. Commissioner, 906 F.3d 429 (6th Cir. 2018). McGowan v. United States, 132 A.F.T.R. 2d 2023-5955 (N.D. Ohio).

9 Treas. Reg. Sec. 20.2042-1(c)(6).

10 Treas. Reg. Sec. 1.62(c)(1)(iv).

11 Treas. Reg. Sec. 1.61-22(b)(3)(ii).

12 Treas. Reg. Sec. 1.61-22(b)(3)(i).

13 Treas. Reg. Sec. 1.61-22(c)(1)(iii).

14 Treas. Reg. Sec. 1.61-22(c)(1)(i).

15 Treas. Reg. Sec. 1.61-22(c)(1).

16 Treas. Reg. Sec. 1.61-22(c)(1)(ii).

17 *See* Treas. Reg. Sec. 20.2042-1(c)(6).

18 *See* Ltr. Ruls. 9511046, 9651030, 9348009, 9204041, and 200728015.

19 Treas. Reg. Sec. 20.2042-1(c)(6).

20 Ltr. Ruls. 9709027, 200822003, 200910002, and 200825011 (for private split-dollar arrangements). Ltr. Ruls. 9348009, 9511046, and 9651030 (for controlling shareholder split-dollar). Ltr. Ruls. 9204041 and 200728015 (for partnership split-dollar).

21 Ltr. Ruls. 9328010, 9328012, 9328017, 9328019, and 9328020.

22 Section 101(a)(2).

23 Ltr. Ruls. 7935127 and 9309021. Ltr. Rul. 9328010 discussed earlier also avoided transfer for value as well as limited policies to one on each insured life by the use of a partnership and grantor trusts.

24 Machacek v. Commissioner, 906 F. 3d 429 (6th Cir. 2018), *non-acq.*, AOD 2021-02. The Tax Court disagreed in De Los Santos v. Commissioner, 156 T.C. 120 (2021).

25 Ltr. Ruls. 9318007, 9413023, 9331009, and 200914019.

26 Treas. Reg. Sec. 1.61-22(f)(2)(ii).

27 Treas. Reg. Sec. 1.83-3(e). Rev. Rul. 60-31, 1960-1 C.B. 174.

28 Casale v. Commissioner, 247 F.2d 440 (2d Cir. 1957), *acq*. Rev. Rul. 59-194, 1959-1 C.B. 65.

29 ERISA Secs. 201(2), 301(a)(3), and 401(a)(1).

30 DOL Adv. Op. 90-14A.

31 DOL Adv. Op. 81-11A. Belka v. Rose Furniture Co., 71 F. Supp. 1240 (D. Md 1983). Belsky v. First national Life Insurance Co., 818 F. 2d 661 (8th Cir. 1987).

32 Miller v. Heller, 915 F. Supp. 651 (S.D. N.Y. 1996).

33 Treas. Reg. Sec. 1.61-22(d)(1). Rev. Rul. 81-198, 1981-2 C.B. 188.

34 Ltr. Rul. 9745019.

35 Treas. Reg. Sec. 1.61-22(c)(ii)(2).

36 Rev. Rul. 82-145, 1982-2 C.B. 213.

37 Rev. Rul. 83-147, 1983-2 C.B. 158.

38 Ltr. Ruls. 200017051 and 200111038.

39 Ltr. Ruls. 9331009, 9318007, 9709027, 9735006, and 200914019.

40 FRRS 5-919.111 (1987), *reconsidered and confirmed* by FRRS 5-917.191 (1988).

41 12 C.F.R. Sec. 221.2.

42 12 C.F.R. Sec. 221.2 and Sec. 221.3(b).

43 12 C.F.R. Sec. 221.3.

44 *See* Ler. Ruls. 9511046 and 9745019.

45 Treas. Reg. Sec. 1.61-22(c)(1)(ii)(A)(2).

46 Treas. Reg. Sec. 1.7872-15(a)(2).

47 Treas. Reg. Sec. 1.7872-15(e). A split-dollar term loan that is payable not later than the death of an individual and that does not provide for sufficient interest is treated as a below-market demand loan and subject to the imputed interest rules of Section 7872. However, a split-dollar gift term loan that does not provide for sufficient interest is treated as a demand loan only for income tax purposes; for gift tax purposes, it is treated as a term loan subject to the imputed interest rules of Section 7872, under Treas. Reg. Sec. 1.7872-15(e)(5)(iv)(D).

48 If the individual's life expectancy is longer than 9 years (up to age 76 years for males or 81 years for females in the one life table), the long-term AFR is used under Treas. Reg. Sec. 1.7872-15(e)(5)(ii)(D). If the insured lives past life expectancy, the loan is considered retired and reissued at the demand rate in effect on the date the original loan was made.

49 Treas. Reg. Sec. 1.7872-15(e)(5). If the loan does not provide for sufficient interest, Section 7872 applies, and the loan is treated as a below-market demand loan. For each year that the loan is outstanding, however, the rate used in the determination of forgone interest is not the blended annual rate but rather is the AFR (based on annual compounding) appropriate for the loan's term as of the month when the loan is made.

50 Treas. Reg. Secs. 1.7872-15(d)(1) and 1.7872-15(j).

51 A Research Institute of America comment notes that most split-dollar loans are non-recourse because the only collateral for the loan is the policy purchased with the loan. Fed. Tax. Coord. H-1629.

52 Treas. Reg. Sec. 1.7872-15(d)(1).

53 Treas. Reg. Sec. 1.7872-15(a)(4)(i). A troublesome aspect of this rule is that there is no apparent provision that would exclude the lender's payment of the borrower's interest obligation from the borrower's income, so that the borrower appears be taxed on both the imputed income under Section 7872 and the actual income from the bonus arrangement—an implausible result. In a donor–donee loan arrangement, the lender would, under this provision, appear to have made two gifts each year—the interest gifted and the interest deemed gifted under Section 7872.

54 As examples of this provision, the Final Split-Dollar Regulations provide that amounts to be paid by an employer under a fully vested non-qualified deferred compensation arrangement that will pay the employee an amount of the interest due under the split-dollar loan will be disregarded. However, a fully vested non-qualified deferred compensation arrangement that provides for payment equal to the employee's salary, which the facts and circumstances show is not related to the employee's interest obligations, will not be disregarded. Treas. Reg. Sec. 1.7872-15(a)(4)(ii).

For any loan in which the parties either expect the lender will forgive the interest or otherwise may be treated as providing the funds for the interest, if interest is stated, the parties would risk triggering the new provision of the regulation applicable to split-dollar loans that treats a loan where interest is to be paid at the AFR as a below market loan.

55 Treas. Reg. Sec. 1.7872-15(h)(1)(iii).

56 Treas. Reg. Sec. 1.7872-15(h)(2). If the loan's stated rate is less than or equal to the appropriate AFR (the AFR used to test the loan for sufficient interest), the amount of interest deemed transferred and retransferred is the excess of the amount of interest payable at the stated rate over the interest actually paid.

57 Section 671 provides in pertinent part:

> Where it is specified in this subpart that the grantor or another person shall be treated as the owner of any portion of the trust, there shall then be included in computing the taxable income and credits of the grantor or the other person those items of income, deductions, and credits against tax of the trust which are attributable to that portion of the trust to the extent that such items would be taken into account under this chapter in computing taxable income or credits against the tax of an individual.

58 Treas. Reg. Sec. 1.671-2(e).

59 Taxable income for a non-grantor trust consists of gross income minus deductions and is generally computed in the same manner as for an individual. Sec. 641.

60 DNI is the maximum amount of distributions that a trust can deduct from its gross income and the maximum amount includible in the beneficiary's gross income. To compute DNI, an initial determination of tentative taxable income is made. Tentative taxable income is the net taxable income to a trust computed as if it were an individual, without consideration of the distribution deduction. After this initial computation is made, various modifications are made pursuant to Section 643. DNI typically does not include capital gains (or losses), which will normally be taxed to (or deductible by) the trust itself.

61 Sections 661 and 651.

62 Sections 662 and 652.

63 Section 673.

64 Section 674.

65 Section 675.

66 Section 676.

67 Section 677.

68 Section 677(a) provides, in part:

> (a) General Rule. – The grantor shall be treated as the owner of any portion of a trust, whether or not he is treated as such owner under section 674, whose income without the approval or consent of any adverse party is, or, in the discretion of the grantor or a nonadverse party, or both, may be . . .
>
> (3) applied to the payment of premiums on polices of insurance on the life of the grantor or the grantor's spouse. . . ."

69 In fact, most insurance trusts would seem to always be grantor trusts because of the broad application of this provision. As discussed later, to intentionally avoid grantor trust status for an insurance trust, the trust would either need to explicitly provide that income be paid out to beneficiaries as earned; that income be segregated in a separate accrued income account and prevented under the terms of the trust from being used to pay premiums; or, preferably, by requiring that any discretionary use of trust income to pay premiums be consented to by an adverse party.

70 Section 167(a)(3) was the predecessor to Section 677(a)(3). It provided, in pertinent part:

> Where any part of the income of a trust . . . is, or in the discretion of the grantor or of any person not having a substantial adverse interest in the disposition of such part of the income may be, applied to the payment of premiums on policies of insurance on the life of the grantor . . . then such part of the income of the trust shall be included in computing the net income of the grantor.

71 *See*, e.g., Rev. Proc. 2016-3, 2016-1 I.R.B. 126, Section 3.01(81).

72 *See,* e.g., Ltr. Ruls. 8007080, 8014078, 8103074, 8112087, 8118051, and 8126047. In general, these rulings stand for the proposition that, as

long as the trustee pays premiums on life insurance policies on the life of grantor or the grantor's spouse under the terms of the trust, then the entire trust will be subject to grantor trust treatment.

73 In two of these rulings, Ltr. Ruls. 8126047 and 8118015, the trustees of each trust were authorized to pay premiums on policies owned by the trust on the grantor's life, first from income of the trust and then from principal. The trustees were also authorized to borrow against the policies if the trust assets were insufficient to pay premiums.

The rulings do not indicate if the trusts had taxable income; instead, the issue was whether each grantor would be treated as owner of the trust he created, for purposes of permitting the grantor to use any deduction otherwise allowed to the trust for the interest expense involved in the policy loan. In both of these rulings, the Service concluded that because the trust instrument provided that income from the trust could be applied toward the payment of premiums on the life of the grantor of the trust at the discretion of the trustees, the grantor would be treated as the owner of "the entire trust." The Service then concluded that any deduction of the trust allowed for an interest expense would be included in computing the taxable income and credits of the grantor of the trust.

Most recently, in FAA 20062701F, the IRS stated that a trust that authorized the use of the entire trust income and principal to pay premiums on a policy or the grantor's life was a wholly grantor trust even though the trust did not yet own any insurance on his life. This seems to be a broad, but potentially helpful, interpretation of current Section 677, making all trusts (insurance trusts or otherwise which contain such a power) wholly grantor trusts. Note that the IRS appeared to be stretching in this ruling to find this trust to be a grantor trust to prevent what was apparently an attempt to move trust income offshore.

74 In reaching this conclusion, the Service relied on Treas. Reg. Sec. 1.671-2(b), which provides, in part, that:

> Since the principal underlying . . . section 671 and following . . . is in general that income of a trust over which the grantor or another person has retained substantial dominion or control should be taxed to the grantor or other person . . . it is ordinarily immaterial whether the income involved constitutes income or corpus for trust accounting purposes. Accordingly, when it is stated in

> the regulations . . . that "income" is attributed to the grantor or another person, the reference, unless specifically limited, is to income determined for tax purposes . . . [w]hen it is intended to emphasize that income for trust accounting purposes . . . is meant, the phrase 'ordinary income' is used.

75 Section 673(a) applies to "a reversionary interest in either the corpus or the income" of a trust. Section 674(a) applies to the "beneficial enjoyment of the corpus or the income" of a trust, and within Section 674, the various subsections either deal with income, corpus, or both income and corpus. *See*, e.g., Section 674(b)(2) (dealing with income only), Section 674(b)(5) (applying only to corpus), and Section 674(b)(4) (dealing with both corpus and income). Finally, Sections 675(1) through (3) refer to administrative powers exercisable over "the corpus or the income of the trust."

76 Note that Ltr. Rul. 8839008 is not the Service's only attempt to broaden the judicially settled meaning of the predecessor to Section 677(a)(3). The assertion in the letter rulings cited in footnote 72, above, that the payment of premiums out of the income of the trust will result in the entire trust being subject to grantor trust treatment is contrary to the case law interpreting the predecessor to Section 677(a)(3), which holds that a trust is a grantor trust *only to the extent of the income used for the payment of premiums*. In fact, the Service's position in those letter rulings directly conflicts with its holding in Rev. Rul. 66-33, 1966-2 C.B. 245, in which the Service deferred to Dunning v. Comm'r, 36 B.T.A. 1222 (1937) and Foster v. Comm'r, 8 T.C. 197 (1947) in concluding that only the amount of income which is used to pay premiums on the policies on the grantor's life would be taxed to the grantor under the predecessor to Section 677(a).

77 Also note that for what it's worth, in these older cases, it was the taxpayer arguing for non-grantor trust status and the Service arguing the opposite; today, those positions would likely be reversed. This role reversal theoretically should not have any effect on the outcome of a given case, but it is possible that a court might view the grantor trust rules as having been enacted to protect the fisc, and not capable of being invoked by a taxpayer.

78 Note that Section 677(a)(3) applies to premiums on policies on the life of the grantor's spouse or on their joint lives (on a survivorship basis) as well.

79 *See*, e.g., Vreeland v. Comm'r, 16 T.C. 1041 (1951).

80 *See*, e.g., Corning v. Comm'r, 104 F.2d 326 (6th Cir. 1939).

81 41 B.T.A. 165 (1940).

82 39 B.T.A. 808 (1939).

83 3 T.C. 579 (1944).

84 40 B.T.A. 233 (1939), *aff'd.*, 116 F.2d 929 (8th Cir. 1941).

85 In light of the argument made by the taxpayer in Rand, *supra* note 84, it should be noted that even if a trust instrument were to specifically prohibit the use of trust income to pay premiums, a court likely would rule that the trust was a grantor trust if trust income was, in fact, used to pay premiums.

86 There are other combinations of the three variables that are neither relevant nor instructive here because they are not possible because premiums cannot be paid on insurance policies that do not exist or deal more directly with the concept of a trust as a mere conduit because the trust is paying premiums on an insurance policy held by another trust. To the extent that one trust pays, out of its income, the premiums on an insurance policy held by another trust, the trust paying the premiums, and not the trust holding the insurance policies, will be treated as a grantor trust. *See,* e.g., Iverson v. Comm'r, 3 T.C. 756 (1944).

87 *See supra* note 81.

88 *See supra* note 82.

89 *See supra* note 83.

90 *See supra* note 84.

91 *See* Corning v. Comm'r, at footnote 80; Stockstrom v. Comm'r, 3 T.C. 664 (1944); Schoellkopf v. McGowan, 43 F.Supp. 568 (W.D.N.Y. 1942); Pillsbury v. Burnet, 67 F.2d 151 (D.C. 1933); Hexter v. Comm'r, 47 B.T.A. 483 (1942); Barbour v. Comm'r, 29 B.T.A. 910 (1939); Dunning v. Comm'r, *supra* note 76; Heffelfinger v. Comm'r, 32 B.T.A. 1232 (1935); Mott v. Comm'r, 30 B.T.A. 1040 (1934); Pillsbury v. Burnet, 12 A.F.T.R. 1364 (1933); Yuengling v. Comm'r, 27 B.T.A. 782 (1933); Philip Meyers, 3 CCH TCM 468 (1944); and Lewis Barker, 2 CCH TCM 797 (1943).

92 It should be noted that although this is the position expressed in the case law, the Service has consistently argued to the contrary—that as long as trust income may be used to pay premiums on a policy on the life of the grantor or his or her spouse, without the consent or approval of an adverse party, the trust is a grantor trust. Accordingly, further steps, as discussed later, should be taken to ensure non-grantor trust treatment under Section 677(a)(3) for an insurance trust, when that is desired (for the reasons discussed later).

93 As defined in Section 672(a).

94 If this provision is used, the trustee would need to obtain such a consent from a beneficiary in advance of actually paying premiums out of trust income.

95 Zaritsky and Leimberg do not reach a conclusion regarding the portion of a trust's income that should be deemed owned by a grantor of a trust when the trustees are authorized to use trust income for premiums on policies on the grantor's life but use only a portion of the trust's income for that purpose. They conclude that support exists for either position, that, is, that all items relating to the trust's income should be deemed owned by the grantor if all of the income could be used to pay premiums or that only an amount equal to the income actually used for premium payments should be deemed owned by the grantor.

96 Under Section 675(4)(C).

97 65 T.C. 92 (1975).

98 *See also* Ltr. Ruls. 9413045 and 9227013.

99 2008-16 I.R.B. 796.

100 The substitution power was, however, often used in these trusts for non-insurance assets, for flexibility purposes, to allow the grantor to move such assets in and out of the trust, without income tax consequences.

101 2011-49 I.R.B. 830.

102 But note the difficulty of determining the fair market value of a policy; is reliance on the interpolated terminal reserve formulation of Treas. Reg. Sec. 25.2512-6(a) adequate for these purposes, or is a formal appraisal (perhaps taking into account the insured's health) required?

103 Under Section 675(2).

104 Note, however, like the Section 677(a)(3) power, this is *not* a power retained by the grantor that can be given up if desired.

105 Because this would impose an income tax burden on the trust or its beneficiaries, which the grantor had been assuming.

106 As noted earlier, obtaining the consent of an adverse party to such a use of any trust income, in advance, should be considered, whenever that provision is used.

107 Note the concern (arguably misplaced in the context of an estate planning transaction) raised by Notice 2007-73, 2007-36 I.R.B. 545, stating that certain forms of investment trusts that allowed grantor trust powers to be "toggled on and off" were "transactions of interest" for tax shelter disclosure and other requirements. Because of this notice and its possible application to grantor trusts used for estate planning, many practitioners require that after a grantor trust power is released or eliminated, it may not be reinstated.

108 *See*, however, the earlier discussion on the deductibility of any such interest payments.

109 Rev. Rul. 85-13, 1985-1 C.B. 184; *but see* Rothstein v. US, 735 F.2d 704 (2d Cir. 1984).

110 However, the grantor will continue to be taxable on income earned by the trust and on gains realized on sales of trust assets.

111 Under the carry-over basis exception of Section 101(a)(2)(A), such a sale, if at the policy's fair market value, would also avoid application of the 3-year "look-back" rule of Section 2035, discussed later, because of the exception for transfers for full and adequate consideration. Under Rev. Rul. 2007-13, 2007-11 I.R.B. 684, a transfer of a policy by the insured or grantor (or even by another grantor trust created by the insured or grantor) to a grantor trust created by the insured or grantor is ignored as a transfer for transfer for value purposes.

Such a sale, however, may not avoid application of the 3-year "look-back" rule of Section 2035 under the exception to Section 2035 for transfers for full and adequate consideration. Section 2035 may still apply even if the policy was sold to the grantor trust for its fair market value because for purposes of Section 2035, the sale price, to be considered full and adequate consideration, may be the full face amount of the policy (which is the amount that would have been includable in the insured's estate had the sale not taken place and the insured had died owning the policy). In such a sale, must the sale price be the amount necessary to replace the policy in the insured's estate for estate tax purposes (its face amount), or is it its gift tax value under the Section 2512 regulations?

Compare TAM 8806004, dealing with a single life policy on the life of the owner (holding that for the sale price to equal full and adequate consideration for purposes of Section 2035, the sale price had to equal the amount necessary to replace the amount that would have been included in the insured's estate for estate tax purposes had the insured died owning the policy) with Ltr. Rul. 9413045, dealing with a survivorship policy owned by one of the insureds (holding that full and adequate consideration for purposes of Section 2035 was the policy's gift tax value, if the insureds were not "near death").

The difference between these holdings appears to be based on the difference between the policies involved—the survivorship policy would presumably have been included in the seller's estate at its fair market value under Section 2031 (which uses the same standards of valuation of policies owned by a decedent on another's life as is used in the gift tax area) even if transferred within 3 years of the owner's death if the other insured were then alive.

112 2004-2 C.B. 6.

113 2007-36 I.R.B. 545.

114 Under Treas. Reg. Sec. 1.6011-4(b)(6) and Sections 6111 and 6112.

115 Assuming the policy is not a survivorship policy.

116 If there are two grantors (because each contributed to the trust or joint or community property was contributed), at the death of the first grantor, half of the trust's grantor status would presumably end, and this half of the trust would then become a complex trust. However, if state law uses a contribution rule and considers a trust with two grantors the same as a joint account, if the deceased grantor contributed all of the property to the grantor trust, the entire trust may lose its grantor trust status.

117 Because the grantor relinquished the power (or all such powers) or it (or they) were revoked by a trust protector or advisor, in either case, acting without fiduciary duties to the trust beneficiaries, under a power granted in the trust instrument.

118 However, the authorities to date treating termination of grantor trust status as a deemed sale of the trust assets in exchange for the trust's liabilities have only dealt with liabilities of the grantor trust to third parties, not to the grantor.

119 As discussed earlier, this requires special drafting of the trust to avoid the application of Section 677(a)(3), which would otherwise make most irrevocable insurance trusts grantor trusts.

120 *See* the discussion in *supra* note 118.

121 Discussed in the text at *infra* note 136.

122 *See* Treas. Reg. Sec. 1.1001-2(c) Example 5; Madorin v. Comm'r, 84 T.C. 667 (1985); Rev. Rul. 77-402, 1977-2 C.B. 222; TAM 200011005, all dealing with termination of grantor trust status during the grantor's life, all dealing with liabilities to third parties, not the grantor, and other than the TAM, all involving trust assets consisting of partnerships with liabilities at the partnership level.

123 As the Blattmachr Article, cited in *infra* note 134, concludes:

> Surprisingly, there is no dispositive authority indicating how the termination of grantor trust status should be treated where, at that time, the trust continues to owe a debt to the grantor. In Reg. 1.1001-2(c), Example 5, the grantor is required to recognize a gain because the property held in trust at the time grantor trust status terminates is encumbered by a debt owed to a third party (not the grantor) that exceeds the grantor's basis in the assets. Clearly, the example was designed to confirm the result in Madorin, 84 TC 667, and Rev. Rul. 77-402, 1977-2 CB 222, in order to prevent taxpayers owning a "burnt-out" tax shelter from disposing of it without recognizing the "recapture" income. Similarly, in TAM 200011005 (which, of course, is not precedential authority), at the time grantor trust status terminated, the trust owed a debt to a third party. And, unlike Example 5, the debt did not arise in a tax-shelter context, but rather as a result of a loan taken by the trustee. The IRS concluded that the transaction was "substantially similar" to the one posited in Example 5 and that, as a result, the grantor had to recognize gain on the excess of the debt over basis. To repeat, however, in neither Example 5 nor the TAM is the debt owed to the grantor. Thus, no extant authority clearly determines the treatment of the grantor in connection with the trust's debt to the grantor where grantor trust status terminates during the grantor's life.

124 At *supra* note 109.

125 Note that the exception does not, by its terms, apply to liabilities disregarded for income tax purposes because of the relationship of the lender and the borrower and the implications of Rev. Rul. 85-13, *supra* note 109. It may be that it was intended to apply to liabilities that were too contingent to be an adjustment to basis.

126 At *supra* note 122.

127 Traditionally, the grantor's basis in the policy was believed to be the total of the premiums paid on the policy, less any non-taxable dividends received (in the case of a participating, whole life policy); more recently, however, perhaps reduced by the cost of the insurance protection provided (however it is determined).

Compare the IRS position in Ltr. Rul. 9443020 with the holding of Gallun v. CIR, 327 F.2d 809 (7th Cir. 1964). In both the letter ruling and in CCA 200501004, the IRS held policy basis was reduced by the value of the insurance protection provided (which the rulings held could, in the absence of other proof, be approximated by the difference between premiums paid and cash value—of course, however, the difference is made up of more than just the cost of insurance charges, most notably the sales commissions and other policy sales expenses that are normally front loaded by deduction from policy cash value in the early years), but in Gallun, policy basis was held to be premiums paid, less non-taxable dividends.

Finally, in Rev. Rul. 2009-13, 2009-21 I.R.B. 1029, the IRS ruled, that, at least in the context of a sale of a policy in a life settlement to a buyer that would not suffer loss on the death of the insured, basis was reduced by the value of the insurance protection provided, without specifying how to determine this value. *Query* if that rule applies, as here, when there is only a deemed sale and it is to the insured's grantor trust for the benefit of his or her family members, not a third party or buyer without an insurable interest in the insured's life.

128 It should be noted that at least one article has suggested that this exception does not apply to exclude liabilities that were originally incurred by the *trust*, rather than the *grantor*, to acquire assets. *See* Deborah V. Dunn & David A. Handler, *Tax Consequences of Outstanding Trust Liabilities When Grantor Status Terminates*, Journal of Taxation, July 2001. Citing TAM 200011005, the article concludes that to fall within the exception of Treas. Reg. Sec. 1.1001-2(a)(3), the liability must have been incurred as a result of the grantor's acquisition of an asset rather than the trust's. It seems, however, that the factual background described in TAM 200011005 may require a narrower application of the ultimate conclusion reached by the IRS than the article suggests.

In TAM 200011005, the grantor transferred appreciated stock to a grantor trust that was administered as two separate GRATs for a short period, with the grantor trust making annuity payments to the grantor. To make the required annuity payments to the grantor, the trustee borrowed money from another trust. On termination of the grantor trust status, the trust disposed of the appreciated stock to remainder trusts for the benefit of the grantor's nephews.

The IRS believed that under Treas. Reg. Sec. 1.1001-2(a), the debts incurred by the grantor trust for purposes of making the annuity payments and secured by the trust assets should be treated as amounts realized by the grantor when the trust ceased to be a grantor trust. The taxpayer argued, in relevant part, that the exception provided by Treas. Reg. Sec. 1.1001-2(a)(3) should apply because the debt was incurred by reason of the trust's acquisition of the stock. The IRS disagreed, stating that language of the exception can only be reasonably read to refer to indebtedness incurred in connection with the grantor's acquisition of the stock. In essence, the debt under these facts was not acquisition indebtedness because neither the grantor nor the trust incurred the debt to *acquire* the stock—instead, the trust incurred the indebtedness because it *held* the stock.

The article correctly summarizes the conclusion of TAM 200011005 that the liabilities must have been incurred as a result of the *grantor's* acquisition of the stock to fall within the intended application of the exception; however, the article fails to discuss the specific facts which lead the IRS to this conclusion in the TAM. Arguably, if the *trust* had incurred the liabilities in connection with *acquiring* the stock, the exception would have applied. Applying this reasoning, the liability incurred by the insurance trust for purposes of acquiring the life insurance policy could be the type of acquisition indebtedness contemplated by Treas. Reg. Sec. 1.1001-2(a)(3); therefore, under this reasoning, any discharge of that indebtedness resulting from termination of the trust's grantor trust status would fall within the exception and would therefore not be included in the amount realized by the grantor for income tax purposes.

129 *See* Rev. Rul. 85-13, at *supra* note 109.

130 At *supra* note 127.

131 For a full discussion of the transfer for value rule and its exceptions, *see* Brody & Leimberg, *Avoiding the Tax Trap of the Transfer for Value Rule*, 32 Estate Planning 3 (Oct. 2005); Brody & Leimberg, *Using a Transactional Analysis to Avoid the Transfer for Value Rule*, 32 Estate Planning 3 (Nov. 2005); 828 T.M., *Insurance Related Compensation.*

132 Treas. Reg. Sec. 1.101-1(b)(4).

133 As discussed in *supra* note 122, the authorities dealing with the income tax consequences on termination of grantor trust status when the trust has outstanding liabilities only relate to termination during the grantor's life. *See* Treas. Reg. Sec. 1.1001-2(c) Example 5; Madorin v. Comm'r, Rev. Rul. 77-402 and TAM 200011005, all at *supra* note 122.

For a point–counterpoint on this issue, compare Gans and Blattmachr, *No Gain at Death*, Trusts and Estates (2010) at 34, with Cantrell, *Gain is Realized at Death*, Trusts and Estates (2010) at 20.

134 *See* Jonathan G. Blattmachr, Mitchell M. Gans, & Hugh H. Jacobson, *Income Tax Effects of Termination of Grantor Trust Status by Reason of the Grantor's Death*, Journal of Taxation, September 2002 ("Blattmachr Article"); Joy Elizabeth Hodge, *On the Death of Dr. Jekyll—The Disposition of Mr. Hyde: The Proper Treatment of an Intentionally Defective Grantor Trust at the Grantor's Death*, 29 Tax Management Estates, Gifts & Trusts Journal 6 (November 11, 2004) ("Hodge Article"); Elliott Manning and Jerome M. Hesch, *Deferred Payment Sales to Grantor Trusts, GRATs and Net Gifts: Income and Transfer Tax Elements*, 24 Tax Management Estates, Gifts and Trust Journal 3 (Jan. 14, 1999). Although these commentators recognize that the Section 1001 regulations provide an exception to the no-gain rule for lifetime transfers of property encumbered by a liability, they emphasize that the regulations contain no indication that the exception to the no-gain rule should be applied to testamentary transfers.

In their view, the exception to the no-gain rule for lifetime transfers is critical in order to prevent potential abuse by taxpayers, whereas there is no necessity for such an exception regarding testamentary transfers. In the absence of the exception, a taxpayer could borrow against an asset up to its value and then gift the asset subject to the liability without recognizing the gain—effectively, converting the asset to cash on a tax-free basis. As the Blattmachr Article articulates, the potential for such abuse makes an exception to the no-gain rule necessary for lifetime transfers. With a testamentary transfer, in contrast, the potential for abuse is much more limited because taxpayers who want to take advantage of the no-gain rule must first die to come within its scope.

The authors of the Blattmachr Article are not certain as to the question of the basis of the assets transferred to the trust on the death of the grantor. Although the authors think that the basis should be governed by

Section 1014, they acknowledge that there are other plausible methods for determining basis. The authors also acknowledge that permitting basis to be determined under Section 1014 is contrary to the conventional understanding of the section that it should apply only where the assets are included in the gross estate. However, in the authors' view, although Section 1014(b)(9) explicitly depends on estate tax inclusion, Section 1014(b)(1) does not. It simply requires that the asset be acquired by bequest, devise, or inheritance or by the decedent's estate from the decedent. Because a grantor trust's assets are deemed to be owned by the grantor for income tax purposes, a good argument can be made, in the authors' view, that assets held in such a trust should be viewed as passing as a bequest or devise when the trust ceases to be a grantor trust at the moment of death.

Alternatively, the authors believe that it is possible to view the trust's acquisition of the assets as a purchase. Under this view, the trust would be treated as having acquired the assets in exchange for the note at the time of the grantor's death. The trust's basis would thus be a cost basis under Section 1012 and would equal the amount of the unpaid principal balance of the note (assuming the note carries adequate stated interest). Another possibility is that basis would be determined under Section 1015 if the acquisition of the assets is viewed as either an *inter vivos* gift or a transaction that is part gift, part sale. According to the authors, if the acquisition is viewed as a "pure gift," then the trustee's basis in the assets would equal the grantor's basis under Section 1015(a) (however, for purposes of computing loss on any subsequent sale, the trustee's basis would be the lesser of the grantor's basis or the fair market value of the asset on the date of the transfer). However, as the authors' point out, it is arguable that Section 1015(b), and not Section 1015(a), should determine basis because of the liability assumed by the trust. Under Section 1015(b), the trustee's basis would be the sum of the grantor's basis and the gain recognized by the grantor on the transfer. Finally, the authors take the position that if the part-gift/part-sale provisions of Treas. Reg. Sec. 1.1015-4 apply, then the trustee's basis would be the greater of the grantor's basis or the amount paid by the trustee.

The Hodge Article similarly posits that because the transfer of assets to the trust on the grantor's death should be deemed a testamentary transfer, the assets should, accordingly, be stepped up in basis under Section 1014(b)(1). The Hodge Article provides other arguments, similar to the Blattmachr Article, in favor of a step-up in basis for the assets transferred to the trust. Under one approach, the basis of the trust assets should be a purchase price basis equal to the amount of the debt at the grantor's death (even though, in the author's view, the transfer would not result in any gain on the grantor's death). Under another approach, the author explains that if contrary to the premise in her article, the grantor's death results in a taxable gain, then it would appear that the assets should be stepped-up by the amount of gain recognized by the grantor's estate (which would not be deemed to be income in respect of a decedent).

135 The authors of the Blattmachr Article and the Hodge Article point to Crane v. Comm'r, 331 U.S. 1 (1947) and subsequent cases to indicate that courts have consistently determined that testamentary transfers from a decedent do not trigger gain. As the authors point out, it was not until Diedrich v. Comm'r, 457 U.S. 191 (1982), that the Supreme Court carved out an exception from the no-gain rule for lifetime gifts which were encumbered by a liability. Although these commentators recognize that the Section 1001 regulations provide an exception to the no-gain rule for lifetime transfers of property encumbered by a liability, they emphasize that the regulations contain no indication that the exception to the no-gain rule should be applied to testamentary transfers.

136 *See* Treas. Reg. Sec. 1.1001-2(c) Example 5; Madorin v. Comm'r, at *supra* note 122. Deborah V. Dunn & David A. Handler, *Tax Consequences of Outstanding Trust Liabilities When Grantor Status Terminates*, *above*; Fred Nicholson, *Sale to a Grantor Controlled Trust: Better Than a GRAT*; 37 Tax Management Memorandum 99 (1996) (in which the author acknowledges that the reasoning in Treas. Reg. Sec. 1.1001-2(c) and the Madorin case at *supra* note 122 may cause the recognition of gain on the grantor's death, to the extent the deemed transfer of assets subject to a liability exceeds the grantor's basis in these assets).

137 Which it would if the theory of Rev. Rul. 2009-13, at *supra* note 127, applied in this deemed sale to reduce the grantor's basis in the policy by the value of the insurance protection provided (however it is determined).

138 As the Blattmachr Article points out, the Treasury recently issued regulations that reveal its views about the no-gain rule in the context of a grantor trust. Section 684, enacted in 1997, provides that as a general rule, a transfer to a foreign trust requires the transferor to recognize all gain inherent in the transferred asset at the time of transfer. The section was clearly designed to apply to lifetime gifts in trust even in the absence of an encumbering liability. Thus, the section contemplates at least a partial qualification of the no-gain rule. Echoing the notion in the domestic (non-foreign) trust setting that transactions or sales between the grantor and a grantor trust are to be disregarded, Section 684(b) provides that Section 684(a) does not apply—and therefore gain is not recognized—when the transfer is made to a grantor trust.

In fleshing out this provision, the regulations address the same questions that arise in the case of a sale to a domestic (US) grantor trust: (1) whether a sale is deemed to occur if the grantor trust status ends during the grantor's lifetime and (2) whether the cessation of grantor trust status by reason of the grantor's death triggers gain under the section.

As to the first issue, Treas. Reg. Sec. 1.684-2(e) provides, as do the regulations under Section 1001, that gain must be recognized when grantor trust status ends. Unlike the regulations under Section 1001, however (which, as indicated, provide that the sale is deemed to occur *at the moment* grantor trust status ceases), Treas. Reg. Sec. 1.684-2(e) creates the fiction that a sale is deemed to occur immediately *before* the cessation of such status. As to the second issue, extending the fiction, the regulations provide that the grantor is deemed to make the sale immediately before death. *See* Treas. Reg. Sec. 1.684-2(e)(2), Example 2.

This approach is inconsistent not only with the rule under Section 1001 but also perhaps with Section 684 itself. Under Section 684(b), no gain is to be recognized as long as the trust remains a grantor trust. And because immediately before the grantor's death, the trust is still a grantor trust, it would appear that the fiction cannot be applied in the event of death without violating subsection (b).

139 At *supra* note 109. Note, however, that the Section 684 regulation provision cited earlier concludes that, nonetheless, gain is recognized, presumably on the decedent's final income tax return, as a deemed transfer.

140 *See* the discussion of these exceptions in the articles cited in *supra* note 131.

141 Interest income may also be imputed under the unstated interest rules of Section 483. The unstated interest rules apply to any payments on the sale or exchange of property that are due more than 6 months after the sale or exchange if some payments are due more than 1 year after the sale or exchange. Section 483 generally applies only if the transaction does not come within the scope of Sections 1273 or 1274. Transactions that are covered by the unstated interest rules of Section 483 rather than the OID rules, include, for example, sales of property for $250,000 or less and sales of a taxpayer's principal residence. *See* Section 1274(c)(3).

142 The term "stated redemption price at maturity" means the sum of all payments due under the debt instrument other than certain qualified interest payments. *See* Section 1273(a)(2).

143 The "imputed principal amount" is equal to the sum of the present value of all payments due under the instrument discounted by the AFR in effect as of the date of sale. *See* Section 1274(b).

144 The basis of the debt instrument in the hands of the holder is increased by the amount of OID that was included in gross income. *See* Section 1272(d)(2).

145 Section 7872 applies to six categories of loans: (1) gift loans, (2) compensation-related loans, (3) corporation-shareholder loans, (4) tax-avoidance loans, (5) any below-market interest loan in which the interest arrangement has a significant effect on either the lender's or borrower's tax liability ("significant effect" loans), and (6) loans to any qualified continuing care facility not exempt under Section 7872(g). *See* Section 7872(c).

146 *See* Section 7872(a)(1).

147 *See* Section 7872(b)(1).

148 *See* Section 7872(b)(2).

149 At *supra* note 109.

150 *See* also Henkel, *Estate Planning and Wealth Preservation: Strategies and Solutions*, at Chapter 30.11[3].

151 Note that in Rev. Rul. 85-13, at *supra* note 109, the IRS refused to follow the contrary decision of the Second Circuit in Rothstein v. United States, at *supra* note 109, in which the court considered a transaction substantially similar to the facts in the ruling in which the grantor claimed an interest deduction on the installment note and a loss on the subsequent sale of the stock to the corporation. The IRS disallowed both deductions. The Second Circuit held that although the grantor must be treated as owner of the trust under the grantor trust provisions, this requires only that the grantor include the trust's items of income, deduction, and credits in his or her own computation of taxable income and that the trust must continue to be viewed as a separate taxpayer. The court therefore held that the sale of the trust assets to the grantor in exchange for an installment note was a bona-fide sale and that the grantor acquired a cost basis in the assets.

152 *See also* the Conference Report to the Deficit Reduction Act of 1984, H. Rep't. 98-861, 98th Cong., 2d. Sess. 1018, in which the conferees clarified that if a taxpayer makes a below-market demand loan to a trust and the loan is treated as a revocable transfer of property for purposes of the grantor trust provisions, then the grantor trust provisions, and not Section 7872, govern because "it would be anomalous to give effect for tax purposes to a loan made by a taxpayer to himself or herself."

153 *See* Deborah V. Dunn & David A. Handler, *Tax Consequences of Outstanding Trust Liabilities when Grantor Status Terminates*, at *supra* note 136, and Jonathan G. Blattmachr, Mitchell M. Gans & Hugh H. Jacobson, *Income Tax Effects of Termination of Grantor Trust Status by Reason of the Grantor's Death*, at *supra* note 134.

154 *See also* Esperti & Peterson, *Irrevocable Trusts: Analysis with Forms*, at Chapter 4.04[4][c].

155 At *supra* note 109.

156 Treas. Reg. Sec. 1.7872-15(a)(2)

157 Professional Services v. CIR., 79 T.C. 888, 915 (1982).

158 *Id.* at 915-16.

159 *See* First National Co. v. CIR., 289 F.2d 861 (6th Cir. 1961).

160 *See* Mountain State Steel Foundries Inc. v. CIR., 284 F.2d 737 (4th Cir. 1960).

161 86 T.C. 848 (1986).

162 *See,* e.g., Denver & Rio Grande Western R.R. Co. v. U.S., 505 F.2d 1266 (Ct. CL. 1974) (obligation payable at rate of 32% of carload freight traffic revenue after movement of 100,000 net tons per year) and Lemery v. CIR., 52 T.C. 367 (1969) (obligation contingent upon business sold showing net profit).

163 *See,* e.g., Brountas v. CIR., 73 T.C. 491 (1979) (payment of note contingent upon discovery of recoverable amounts of oil or gas) and Gibson Products Co. v. United States, 637 F. 2d 1041 (5th Cir. 1981) (same).

164 *Waddell* at 909.

165 *Id.* at 911.

166 *See* Hambuechen v. CIR., 43 TC 90, 98 (1964).

167 Gilbert v. CIR., 248 F.2d 399, 402 (2nd Cir. 1957); *See also* GCM 36702 (April 12, 1976).

168 *See* Hambuechen v. CIR., at *supra* note 166; *also see* Federal Projects, Inc. v. CIR., T.C.M. 1987-202 (1987).

169 *See,* e.g., Estate of Kelley v. CIR., 63 T.C. 321 (1974) (*nonacq.*, 1977-2 C.B. 2); Haygood v. CIR., 42 T.C. 936 (1964) (1965-1 C.B. 4, *withdrawn and nonacq. substituted* 1977-2 C.B. 2); Story v. CIR., 38 T.C. 936 (1962). *See also* Wilson v. CIR., 1992-40 T.C.M., (holding that a self-cancelling note was valid indebtedness, based on the borrower's intent to repay).

170 T.C.M. 1989-55 at 1690.

171 Rev. Rul. 77-299, 1977-2 C.B. 343.

172 29 T.C. 730 (1958).

173 *Id.* at 736.

174 The right to obtain an interest in the policy under subrogation or similar rights, provided either under the loan documents or state law (or both) would be an incident of ownership in the policy, and would need to be specifically negated in the documents.

175 If the grantor did become entitled to a share in the proceeds, as subrogee, then that share of the proceeds would obviously be included in the insured's estate.

176 *See* Pritchard v. United States, 397 F.2d 60 (5th Cir. 1968).

177 *See supra* note 176.

178 *See,* e.g., Estate of Goodwyn v. Comm'r, T.C. Memo 1973-153; Estate of Glade v. Comm'r, T.C. Memo 1978-316; and Bintliff v. United States, 462 F.2d 403 (5th Cir. 1972). To avoid any risk of this argument, a policy owned by an irrevocable insurance trust created by the insured should not be used as security for the insured's obligations to a third party.

179 The ruling did not discuss whether the insured had retained a security interest in the policy for his loan; if he had, it presumably would have to have been a "restricted" assignment to avoid giving the insured incidents of ownership in the policy. *See* Ltr. Rul. 9511046, *above*.

180 893 F.2d 237 (10th Cir. 1989).

181 918 F.2d 1263 (6th Cir. 1990).

182 *See supra* note 180.

183 *Id.*

184 The same analysis would apply to the consequences of a guarantee and a pledge of assets as security for a loan, not accompanied by a guarantee.

185 Note the issue of the potential estate tax consequences of any subrogation rights held by the insured under the guarantee agreement.

186 The leading case supporting the proposition that a shareholder could increase his or her basis by the amount of a loan guaranteed by the shareholder is Selfe v. United States, 778 F.2d 769 (11th Cir. 1985). In *Selfe*, the Eleventh Circuit remanded for a determination by the District Court to determine whether the taxpayer's personal guarantee on a loan to her business would increase the basis in her stock where the lender looked to the shareholder for repayment. The shareholder obtained a loan in her name to start her retail clothing business. The business was later incorporated. When the shareholders elected to have the corporation taxed as an S corporation, the loans originally made to the taxpayer were transferred to the corporation. The shareholder then personally guaranteed the loans and pledged other assets to the bank. The decision in *Selfe* has not been followed by the remaining courts.

The decision in Selfe has been followed where the court determines that the debtor is actually the shareholder. *See*, Bolding v. Comm'r, 117 F.3d 270 (5th Cir. 1997) (holding that S corporation shareholder was entitled to increase his basis where bank loaned funds directly to shareholder, bank looked to shareholder to repay loans, and proceeds were contributed to corporation; taxpayer, as debtor, was not asked to "guarantee" loans of corporation). *But see* Nigh, et al. v. Comr., 60 T.C.M. 91 (1990) (holding that S corporation shareholders were not entitled to increase basis when they were co-makers of loan rather than guarantors).

187 *See*, Leavitt Est. v. Comm'r., 90 T.C. 206 (1988), *aff'd*, 875 F.2d 420 (4th Cir. 1989); Harris v. United States, 902 F.2d 439 (5th Cir. 1990); Brown v. Comm'r., 706 F.2d 755 (6th Cir. 1983); Sleiman v. Comm'r., 187 F.3d 1352 (11th Cir. 1999); and Calcutt v. Comm'r., 91 T.C. 14 (1988).

188 81 Va. L. Rev. 223 (February 1995).The article "Shareholder Guarantees of S Corporation Debt: Matching the Tax Consequences with Economic Reality" notes the following:

> The Internal Revenue Service has recently struggled to develop its position on the valuation of shareholder guarantees. In 1991, the Service surprised the legal community when it issued a

private letter ruling stating that a parent's guarantee of a child's debt should be considered a gift at the time the guarantee is made. The Service did not indicate in the ruling whether the gift guarantee would be valued at the face amount of the loan or by a different method. When practitioners inquired about the correct application of the private letter ruling, for three years the Service would only respond that it was reevaluating its position on gift guarantees. By the middle of 1993, several members of Congress had become interested in applying a legislative solution to the guarantee issue posed by the Service. Senator Daniel K. Akaka of Hawaii proposed the addition of a subsection to section 2056(b) of the code that would value gift guaranties not on the face value of the indebtedness guaranteed but on the likelihood that the guarantor would be called to perform on the guarantee (a valuation method). On December 1, 1993, possibly because of the congressional pressure *and persistent fear that its position in the gift guarantee area might trigger a new examination of the S corporation shareholder guarantee controversy (which would cause greater overall revenue losses to the Service), the Service withdrew the gift guarantee sections of the December 21, 1990 letter ruling [Ltr. Rul. 9113009] without explanation* (emphasis added).

189 Another possible way to avoid or mitigate this issue would be to have the trust pay the grantor an arm's length fee (perhaps determined by appraisal or by simple reference to a bank's letter of credit fee); this would seem to make the guarantee a business arrangement and therefore non-donative. Because the trust would normally be a grantor trust from the point of view of the donor-guarantor, the guarantee fee would not be income to the donor nor deductible by the trust. If the grantor had to gift the amount of the guarantee to the trust to allow the trust to pay the fee, that amount would be a gift for gift tax purposes.

190 Cahill v. CIR, TCM 2018-84, a Memorandum Decision, denying the Estate's Motion for Summary Judgment.

191 Which was governed by Treas. Reg. Sec. 1.61-22; split-dollar loan regime transactions, on the other hand, are governed by Treas. Reg. Sec. 1.7872-15 rather than by Treas. Reg. Sec. 1.61-22.

192 See Frazee v. CIR, 98 T.C. 554 (1992) and True v. CIR, T.C.M. 2001-167, both analogous intra-family installment sale (not loan)

transactions, in which the Tax Court held that the notes received by the sellers were to be valued, on issuance, under Section 7872, not under the usual willing buyer/willing seller valuation standard.

In *Frazee*, the Tax Court stated: "Pursuant Section 7872(b), the amount of the gift equals the excess of the amount loaned over the present value of all payments which are required under the terms of the loan. The value of the promissory note, therefore, must be recomputed using the Federal rate for long-term loans, compounded semiannually, with quarterly payments at the time petitioners conveyed the property to their children. . . . We find it anomalous that respondent urges as her primary position the application of Section 7872, which is more favorable to the taxpayer than the traditional fair market value approach, but we heartily welcome the concept."

Does the Tax Court's welcoming comment about the use of Section 7872 to value notes received in an installment sale transaction reflect a recognition of the practical difficulties of having to appraise notes received in intra-family loan or sale transactions to comply with the usual willing buyer/willing seller standard?

193 Prop. Treas. Reg. Sec. 25.7872-1 provides that if the amount loaned exceeds the present value of the payments to be made, that excess is a gift from the lender to the borrower for Federal gift tax purposes; implying that a loan which provides for AFR interest does not result in a gift by the lender to the borrower for Federal gift tax purposes. See also the Preamble to Treas. Reg. Sec. 1.7872-15 implying that accepting a note issued for a loan which would be valued in a willing buyer–willing seller scenario at less than its face amount does not result in a gift by the lender to the borrower for federal gift tax purposes.

194 Although for transfers of the note during life or at death, a subjective, willing buyer–willing seller standard would be used to value the note for Federal transfer tax purposes. See Strauss and Hesch, "A Noteworthy Dichotomy: Valuation of Intra Family Notes for Transfer Tax Purposes," 45 *Tax Management Estates, Gifts and Trusts Journal* 4 (2020).

195 Note that although Section 2036(a) itself uses the word "sale," in describing the exception, Treas, Reg. Sec. 20.2036-1 uses the broader word "transfer," which seems more appropriate in a loan transaction.

196 See Treas. Reg. Sec. 1.7872-15(e)(4). The attached Appendix provides a more detailed analysis of this issue.

197 The Preamble to the Section 1.7872-15 Regulations recognizes that in the early years of a split-dollar loan, the value of the policy will be lower than the amount loaned, with no suggestion that because of that difference, the loan could be for less than adequate and full consideration and therefore would be considered a gift for Federal gift tax purposes.

198 40 T.C. 714 (1963).

199 80 AFTR 2d 97-5085 (5th Cir. 1997).

200 84 AFTR 2d 99-5227 (9th Cir. 1999).

201 324 U.S. 308 (1945).

202 308 U.S. 39 (1939).

203 The Court stated: "The split-dollar agreements taken as a whole clearly restrict decedent's right to terminate the agreements and withdraw his investment. . . ."

Note that despite the *Cahill* court's reasoning that Section 2703(a) applied in that case because the donor could not "use" what the Court called his "investment"—the amount he had advanced to the trust, in a loan regime transaction, the "property" for Section 2703 purposes is what was owned at death—the note—not what was transferred during life—the amount loaned, nor what was purchased by the borrower with the loan proceeds—the policy.

204 See Treas. Reg. Sec. 1.7872-15(a)(2)(i)(B).

205 Unlike an economic benefit arrangement, in which termination of the agreement requires the trust to repay the premium provider what he or she is owed, which would require the trust to transfer the policy to the premium provider, in a loan regime arrangement, termination of the agreement does not require the trust to repay the lender under the terms of the note.

206 Treas. Reg. Sec. 1.61-22(c)(1)(ii)(A). In Estate of Morrissette v. Commissioner, 166 T.C. No. 11 (April 13, 2016), the IRS argued that a single premium intergenerational split dollar arrangement was a loan regime and not an economic benefit regime non-equity split-dollar arrangement. The Tax Court rejected IRS arguments that in addition to current life insurance protection, the ILITs benefited from access to cash value and lump sum pre-payment of economic benefits, generated by the single premium.

207 Treas. Reg. Sec. 1.61-22(c)(1)(ii)(B)(2). This is discussed in more detail at V.G. later.

208 Treas. Reg. Sec. 1.61-22(d)(1).

209 Treas. Reg. Sec. 1.61-22(f)(2)(i).

210 Treas. Reg. Sec. 1.61-22(g)(4)(iii).

211 Final Split-Dollar Arrangements Regulations, at C.3.a., T.D. 9092, I.R.B. 2003-160. (the "2003 Final Split-Dollar Regulations Preamble")

212 Treas. Reg. Sec. 1.61-22(g)(1).

213 Treas. Reg. Sec. 1.61-22(d)(5)(i)(ii).

214 Treas. Reg. Sec. 1.61-22(d)(5)(iii).

215 Treas. Reg. Sec. 1.61-22(d)(3)(i).

216 Treas. Reg. Sec. 1.61-22(d)(3)(ii).

217 2002-1 C.B. 398.

218 2001-5 I.R.B. 459.

219 Ltr. Rul. 8547006.

220 Rev. Rul. 67-154, 1967-1 C.B. 11.

221 IRS Split-Dollar Life Insurance Audit Technique Guide (3-2005).

222 This letter was from Norman Greenberg, Chief, General Actuarial Branch of the IRS, to Morton Greenberg, Advanced Underwriting Director and Counsel, the Manufacturers Life Insurance Company. Because of the names of the parties to the letter, it is often referred to as the "Greenberg to Greenberg letter."

223 Ltr. Rul. 9709027.

224 *See* Ltr. Rul. 200910002.

225 *Id.*

226 2003 Final Split-Dollar Regulations Preamble at 3.a.

227 Treas. Reg. Sec. 1.61-22(d)(4)(ii).

228 Treas. Reg. Sec. 1.61-22(d)(6), Ex. 1.

229 2003 Final Split-Dollar Regulations Preamble at 3.a.

230 At *supra* note 206.

231 Note that in a non-equity split-dollar arrangement, such right of cash value access would disqualify the economic benefit regime resulting in a loan regime arrangement.

232 The *Morrissette* case involved an intergenerational split-dollar arrangement (discussed more fully at V.J.). Such a transfer at grantor's death would have dissolved the split-dollar arrangement by merger. The transfer could result in a significant discount for estate tax purposes because of the intergenerational contract restrictions, but the *Morrissette* court did not have the valuation issues before it.

233 2003 Final Split-Dollar Regulations Preamble at 3.a.; Treas. Reg. Sec. 1.61-22(d)(6), Ex. 2. *Also see* Our Country Home Enterprises, Inc. v. Commissioner; 145 T.C. 1 (2015), De Los Santos v. Commissioner, T.C. Memo 2018-155 (2018); and McGowan v. United States, 132 A.F.T.R 2d 2023-5955 (N.D. Ohio) in which split-dollar policies owned by a welfare benefit trust denied access to the employer and employer creditors.

234 Treas. Reg. Sec. 1.61-22(e)(1).

235 Treas. Reg. Sec. 1.61-22(h), Ex.7.

236 Treas. Reg. Sec. 1.61-22(e)(3).

237 Treas. Reg. Sec. 1.61-22(e)(2).

238 Treas. Reg. Sec. 1.61-22(h) Ex. 8.

239 The Tax Court summarily dismissed another IRS argument that the prepayment of premiums created a reverse split-dollar arrangement described in Notice 2002-59, 2002-2 C.B.481. The court concluded that the *Morrissette* arrangement bore no resemblance to reverse split-dollar arrangements that would have involved excessive premiums paid by the grantor's revocable trust to the cash value benefit of the ILITs. Here the revocable trust paid reasonable premiums and kept full control of the policy cash value.

240 Treas. Reg. Sec. 1.61-22(f)(3)(i).

241 *Id.*

242 2003 Final Split-Dollar Regulations Preamble at 3.b.

243 Treas. Reg. Sec. 1.61-22(f)(3)(ii).

244 Treas. Reg. Sec. 1.61-22(f)(2)(ii).

245 2003 Final Split-Dollar Regulations Preamble at 3.a.

246 1985-1 C.B. 184.

247 Treas. Reg. Sec. 1.61-22(f)(2)(ii).

248 Treas. Reg. Sec. 1.61-22(f)(2)(i).

249 *Id.* Sec. 264(a)(1).

250 Treas. Reg. Sec. 1.61-22(g)(1).

251 Treas. Reg. Sec. 1.61-22(g)(3).

252 Treas. Reg. Sec. 1.61-22(h), Ex. 5.

253 Treas. Reg. Sec. 1.61-22(g)(2).

254 Treas. Reg. Sec. 1.83-3(e).

255 Treas. Reg. Sec. 1.61-22(d)(4)(i).

256 Treas. Reg. Sec. 1.83-3(e).

257 2005-17 I.R.B. 962.

258 Treas. Reg. Sec. 1.61-22(g)(2).

259 Q/A 10, 1989-1 C.B. 662.

260 Treas. Reg. Sec. 1.402(a)-1(a)(2).

261 Treas. Reg. Sec. 1.72-16(c)(2)(h).

262 Treas. Reg. Sec. 1.61-22(g)(2). *Also see* Final Split-Dollar Regulations Preamble at 5 and Rev. Rul. 81-198, 1981-2 C.B. 188. *Also see* Final Split-Dollar Regulations, Background and Explanation of Provisions, 5, T.D. 9092, I.R.B. 2003-46 and Rev. Rul., 81-198, 1981-2 C.B. 188.

263 *See* Treas. Reg. Sec. 25.2512-6(a), Ex. 4.

264 Policies where premiums are being paid by cash value draws, dividends, or surrender of paid up additions fall outside of paid-up policies because policy premiums are still being paid, although internally within the policy.

265 Treas. Reg. Sec. 25.2512-6(a), Ex. 3. *See* United States v. Ryerson, 312 U.S. 260 (1941).

266 Rev. Rul. 78-137, 1978-1 C.B. 280.

267 Treas. Reg. Sec. 25-2512-6(a).

268 Estate of Pritchard v. Comm'r, 4 T.C. 204 (1944).

269 *Id.*

270 Ltr. Rul. 9413045.

271 Treas. Reg. Sec. 1.61-22(c)(1)(ii)(B).

272 Treas. Reg. Sec. 1.61-22(c)(1)(ii)(B)(1).

273 Donald O. Jansen & Charles L. Ratner, Discount private split-dollar: Does it work? *Trusts & Estates*, May 2008 at 19.

274 At *supra* note 206.

275 In Estate of Marion Levine v. Commissioner, Tax Court Docket No. 9345-15 (July 13, 2016), Tax Court Judge Mark V. Holmes entered an order granting the taxpayer's motion for summary judgement dismissing an IRS challenge of another lump sum premium payment non-equity intergenerational split dollar arrangement. The court concluded that the three year statute of limitations had run on the split-dollar arrangement that the taxpayer disclosed on a gift tax return for the year it was entered into. Although the court did not get to the substantive IRS arguments, apparently the IRS had argued that the split-dollar arrangement was a gift or, at least, was a below-market loan regime split dollar arrangement like it argued in *Morrissette*. In his one page order, the judge cited *Morrissette* as controlling.

276 Rev. Rul. 2008-50, 2008-45 I.R.B. 1098.

277 Section 101(a)(2).

278 Rev. Rul. 78-420, 1978-2 C.B. 67; TAM 9604001. Such premium payments are gifts under Treas. Reg. Sec. 25.2511-1(h)(8).

279 2003 Final Split-Dollar Regulations Preamble at 3.a.

280 There are several private letter rulings involving private non-equity split-dollar when the ILIT paid the term premium holding there was no gift. Ltr. Ruls. 200848002, 200822003, and 200910002.

281 *See* the discussion in Part V.C. of this book.

282 Treas. Reg. Sec. 1.61-22(d)(1).

283 Rev. Rul. 81-198, 1981-2 C.B. 188 citing Treas. Reg. Sec. 25.2512-6.

284 2003 Final Split-Dollar Regulations Preamble at 5.

285 Treas. Reg. Sec. 1.61-22(g)(1)(2). Treas. Reg. Sec. 25.2512-6(a). *See* Article V.F.2 of this book for more details.

286 2003 Final Split-Dollar Regulations Preamble at 5.

287 Ltr. Rul. 9026041 (employer–employee reverse split-dollar, employee had incidents of ownership, all proceeds included in insured's estate, deduction for proceeds paid to the employer under the contract).

288 Rev. Rul. 79-129, 1979-1 C.B. 306. (In a private split-dollar arrangement, the insured could borrow cash value as an incident of ownership, with no debt deduction for the non-owner's interest in the policy.)

289 Treas. Reg. Sec. 1.61-22(c)(1)(i).

290 Ltr. Ruls. 200825011 and 200910002.

291 Ltr. Ruls. 200910002 and 200825011. Both rulings involved so-called "bare bones" collateral assignments with all incidents of ownership possessed by the ILIT. The IRS ruled that the donor had no incidents of ownership and only the cash value payable to the donor's estate was included in the donor's gross estate under Section 2042(1). In Ltr. Rul. 200825011, the donor had the unilateral right to terminate the split-dollar arrangement so that the donor could access the cash value. This might be an incident of ownership, although it was not raised by the IRS in the private ruling. It is best to avoid such termination power by the donor until there is official authority on this subject.

292 Treas. Reg. Sec. 20.2042-1(c)(6).

293 Estate of Levy v. Comm'r, 70 T.C. 873 (1978). Estate of Dimen v. Comm'r, 72 T.C. 198 (1979), *aff'd* 633 F.2d 203 (2d Cir, 1980) (*unpublished opinion*). Rev. Rul. 82-145, 1982-2 C.B. 213.

294 Ltr. Ruls. 951030, 9651030, 9348009, 9294941, and 200728015.

295 Treas. Reg. Sec. 1.61-22(a)(1)(iv).

296 1983-2 C.B. 158.

297 Ltr. Rul. 200017051.

298 Ltr. Rul. 200111038.

299 Treas. Reg. Sec. 20.2042-1(c)(6).

300 Estate of Knipp v. Comm'r, 25 T.C. 153 (1955*), aff'd on other grounds*, 244 F.2d 436 (4th Cir. 1956), *cert. denied*, 355 U.S. 827 (1957), *acq. in result*, 1959-1 C.B. 4.

301 *Id.* at 168-69.

302 G.C. Memo. 39,034 (1983).

303 T.C. Memo 1977-0268.

304 25 T.C. 153, 168.

305 158 T.C. No.2 (2022).

306 T.C. Memo 2018-84.

307 T.C. Memo. 2021-60.

308 T.C. Memo. 2018-84.

309 T.C. Memo. 21-60.

310 T.C. Memo. 2021-60.

311 Treas. Reg. Secs. 1.61-22, 1.83(e), 1.83-6(a)(5), 1.301-1(q), and 1.7872-15.

312 1964-2 C.B. 11.

313 2003-40 I.R.B. 696

314 *See also* IRS Notices 2001-10, 2001-5 I.R.B. 459 and 2002-8, 2002-1 I.R.B. 348, which allow the parties—on an elective basis (subject to some restrictions)—to apply Section 7872 to these arrangements, and the Final Split-Dollar Regulations, which will generally mandate that treatment for most post-Final Regulation collateral assignment (but not endorsement) arrangements.

315 *See,* e.g., TAM 199918060. *See also* Healy v. U.S. 843 F. Supp. 562 (DC-SD 1994).

316 2002-1 C.B. 398 (2002).

317 1978-2 C.B. 67.

318 1981-2 C.B. 188.

319 At *supra* note 316.

320 1955-2 C.B. 228 (1955).

321 1964-2 C.B. 11 (1964).

322 1966-1 C.B. 12 (1966).

323 At *supra* note 320.

324 At *supra* note 322.

325 1967-1 C.B. 11.

326 Under Prop. Treas. Reg. Sec. 1.7872-10(a)(2).

327 Under Section 7872(f)(5) and Prop. Treas. Reg. Secs. 1.7872-10(a)(1) and (5).

328 Under Section 7872(a)(2) and Prop. Treas. Reg. Sec. 1.7872-6.

329 Under Section 7872(b)(1).

330 Prop. Treas. Reg. Sec. 1.7872-4(g).

331 1985-1 C.B. 184.

332 At *supra* note 314.

333 At *supra* note 320.

334 *See supra* note 321.

335 At *supra* note 322.

336 1982-02 C.B. 213.

337 Section 409A(a)(2)-(4).

338 Section 409A(b)(1)-(3).

339 Sections 409(9)(1) and 409A (b)(4)-(5).

340 Treas. Reg. Sec. 1.409A-6(a)(1)(ii).

341 Preamble II(H), Prop. Reg. Sec. 409A, 2005-2 C.B. 786 (the "2005 Proposed 409A Regulation Preamble").

342 2007-17 I.R.B. 996.

343 Sec. 409A(d)(1)(B), Treas. Reg. Sec. 1.409A-1(a)(5) and Notice 2007-34, 2007-17 I.R.B. 996, III.B.

344 Notice 2007-34, *supra,* III.B.

345 Treas. Reg. Sec. 1.409A-1(b)(4); Notice 2007-34, *supra*, III.B.

346 Treas. Reg. Sec. 1.61-22(d)(2)(ii)-(iii).

347 *See* Treas. Reg. Sec. 1.61-22(d)(6), Ex. 1.

348 Treas. Reg. Sec. 1.61-22(d)(2)(ii).

349 Treas. Reg. Sec. 1.61-22(d)(4)(ii).

350 2005 Proposed Section 409A Regulation Preamble at II.H.

351 Notice 2007-34, *supra*, III.c.

352 Notice 2007-34, *supra*, III.c.

353 Section 61(a)(1). The Preamble to the Final Split-Dollar Regulations states that loan treatment under Treas. Reg. Sec. 1.7872-15(a)(2) will be denied "if the arrangement does not provide for repayment by the owner to the non-owner." 2003 Final Split-Dollar Regulations Preamble at 4.a.

354 Section 61(a)(12). However, there is no income if the discharge from indebtedness is the result of the debtor's discharge through bankruptcy or insolvency. Section 108(a).

355 *See* TAM 200040004. This is a disturbing IRS ruling. The fatal flaw was a guaranteed bonus from the employer equal to each note installment payment plus interest. The TAM noted that the employee was liable for the balance due on the loan if he terminated employment, but the ruling did not consider this to be personal liability by the employee; "this repayment obligation appears to be more in the nature of liquidated damages for breach of the employment contract." Some commentators think that forgivable loans are currently taxable disguised salary advances and not real loans even without a bonus arrangement. Denha, "The Tax Impact of Employer Loans to Employees," blog. Alverez & Marsal, "Warning—Employee Loans Could Have Adverse Tax Consequences," blog, Oct. 3, 2012.

356 "The rights of the person to compensation are subject to a substantial risk of forfeiture if the person's rights to such compensation are conditioned upon the future performance of substantial services by any individual." Section 409A(d)(4).

357 Treas. Reg. Sec. 1.409A-1(b)(4)(i)(A).

358 2005 Proposed 409A Regulation Preamble at II.H.

359 Notice 2007-34, *supra*, III.C.

360 Treas. Reg. Sec. 1.409A-6(a)(1)(i).

361 Treas. Reg. Sec. 1.409A-6(a)(4)(i).

362 Treas. Reg. Secs. 1.409A-6(a)(2) and 1.409A-6(a)(1)(ii).

363 Treas. Reg. Sec. 1.409A-6(a)(2).

364 The IRS granted a transition period to amend deferred compensation plans to comply with Section 409A, but it expired on December 31, 2008. Notice 2007-78, 2007-41 I.R.B. 780. There is a special transition rule for split-dollar plans covered by Notice 2002-8, 2002-1 C.B. 398. *See* Notice 2007-34, *supra*, II.C.

365 2007-17 I.R.B. 996.

366 Notice 2007-34, *supra*, III.A.2.

367 Notice 2007-34, *supra,* III.A.2.

368 *See* Part VI of this book.

369 Notice 2002-34, *supra*, at III.D.1.

370 Notice 2002-8, *supra,* at VI.

371 In two companion cases with facts involving grandfathered equity split-dollar, the Tax Court held against the taxpayer on another significant issue with no discussion of taxation of the equity. Neff v. Comm'r and Jensen v. Comm'r, T.C. Memo 2012-244. There are several possible explanations as to why the IRS did not raise the issue—it was missed, the equity income was just a fraction of the income from the other issue and wasn't worth the bother, or the IRS consciously decided not to pursue it. It isn't clear, and accordingly, the cases aren't precedent one way or the other.

372 Notice 2007-34, *supra*, III.D.2. There is no deadline in the Notice for adoption of the required amendments. However, many practitioners believe that the transition rule for Notice 2007-34 expired with the other split-dollar transition rules either at December 31, 2007, under Notice 2006-79, 2006-43 I.R.B. 763 or at December 31, 2008, under Notice 2007-89, 2007-46 I.R.B. 990.

373 Notice 2007-34, *supra*, III.D.1.

Index

F

R

S

T